# Is There Life After Death?

# Is There Life After Death?

Other books in the At Issue series:

# Is There Life After Death?

Rebecca K. O'Connor, *Book Editor*

Bruce Glassman, *Vice President*
Bonnie Szumski, *Publisher*
Helen Cothran, *Managing Editor*

**GREENHAVEN PRESS**
*An imprint of Thomson Gale, a part of The Thomson Corporation*

Detroit • New York • San Francisco • San Diego • New Haven, Conn.
Waterville, Maine • London • Munich

*For more information, contact*
Greenhaven Press
27500 Drake Rd.
Farmington Hills, MI 48331-3535
Or you can visit our Internet site at http://www.gale.com

| LIBRARY OF CONGRESS CATALOGING-IN-PUBLICATION DATA |
| --- |
| Is there life after death? / Rebecca K. O'Connor, book editor. |
|    p. cm. — (At issue) |
| Includes bibliographical references and index. |
| ISBN 0-7377-2406-4 (lib. : alk. paper) — ISBN 0-7377-2407-2 (pbk. : alk. paper) |
|    1. Future life. I. O'Connor, Rebecca K. II. At issue (San Diego, Calif.) |
| BL535.I8  2005 |
| 133.9'01'3—dc22                                                  2004052399 |

# Contents

# Introduction

Scientists to date have been unable to use scientific means to prove that the soul or some other form of identity survives death. Stories of encounters with spirits are common, yet no one has been able to confirm that the ghosts of the deceased exist. Many people have also claimed to witness the afterlife during near death experiences, but those experiences are not scientific proof that there is a soul that leaves the body after death. Despite this lack of evidence about the afterlife, the number of Americans who believe in an afterlife is growing.

According to a 2003 Harris poll, 84 percent of Americans believe in the survival of the soul. Because of this high percentage, the poll has received a lot of media attention. In Canada, for example, only 54.7 percent of people believe in life after death.

In a modern world whose development has been greatly based on scientific principles, it is surprising that an increasing number of Americans would believe in an afterlife that has been impossible to prove. Even some religious leaders have not expected so many Americans to develop a belief in life after death. Andrew Greeley, a popular author and Catholic priest, noted in 2001 that theoretically, "Belief in a supernatural reality will slowly erode as educational levels rise and the impact of scientific thinking expands." However, this has not been the case. Not only is the percentage of believers high, but it increased 24 percent between 1972 and 2001.

Many Americans believe in an afterlife because the various religions they practice teach that life after death exists. All religions teach that there is an immortal soul and that after humans die, the soul lives on. Some religions such as Catholicism hold that the soul leaves the body and eventually enters a heaven or a hell. Other religions such as Hinduism teach that souls return to earth in another form.

Religious belief, however, does not completely account for the large numbers of Americans who believe in life after death. Some people argue that popular culture strongly influences Americans' belief in the afterlife. Americans may develop their beliefs from watching television or movies, reading books, or listening to music, rather than from going to church. As Terry Mattingly, an associate professor of mass media and religion at Palm Beach Atlantic University states, "Today, if people want to find out about eternity, they are just as likely—or more likely— to go to a multiplex or the mall, instead of church."

Cable television has introduced many Americans to the belief that the dead are still close enough to converse with their loved ones. John Edward's cable show *Crossing Over* has become one of the most popular shows on the Sci Fi channel. In front of a studio audience, Edward describes the messages he says he is receiving from the dead and passes on important information to the living. The interest that many Americans have in the show demonstrates the willingness of many people to believe that there is an afterlife. According to writer Matt Nisbet, "Since its premiere, 'Crossing Over' has increased Sci Fi Channel ratings 33% over the same time period for the previous year, to a daily average of 533,000 households." Edward's popularity has also grown because of the books he has written about communicating with the dead, including *One Last Time: A Psychic Medium Speaks to Those We Have Loved and Lost.*

Americans are reading other books, such as Mitch Albom's best-selling novel *The Five People You Meet in Heaven* to get ideas about the afterlife. In Albom's vision of life after death, each person encounters five people in heaven whose lives they have affected during their own time on earth. Albom states, "It isn't researched first-person. I didn't go there and come back. But it is my hope that if heaven doesn't work exactly like that, the spirit is like that." His book made the top five on the *New York Times* best-seller lists for several months during 2004 indicating how many Americans are looking to authors for inspiration and descriptions of a possible afterlife. Another recent popular book about the afterlife is *A Travel Guide to Heaven* by Anthony DeStefano, who states that his book is Christian-based nonfiction. The 208-page book describes heaven as a real place where there will be friends and family, cities, and animals. Like Albom, DeStefano does not claim to have seen the afterlife, but believes in his vision of eternity. He states, "I would bet my life that I'll have a body in heaven and there will be colors in heaven." Whether or not he is correct, the book debuted in 2003 as number one on Amazon.com's "Movers and Shakers" list and number seven on its list of best sellers. It has also been reprinted three times.

Another way popular culture is shaping Americans' belief is through the Internet, which contains thousands of Web sites about life after death. One of the most interesting afterlife Web sites is AfterlifeTelegrams.com, which offers people the opportunity to send messages through the terminally ill to deceased loved ones. AfterlifeTelegrams.com offers this service for five dollars per word. Terminally ill individuals memorize the messages to be delivered, and upon their death the fee is used for funeral expenses or goes to their family or a charity. The site, which has been available since 2003, has garnered a lot of media attention and has been the topic of articles in the *Washington Post*, the *Chicago Tribune*, and *Harper's* magazine.

Although many Americans believe strongly that there is an afterlife, their visions of it vary greatly. As well, many people continue to argue that there is not enough evidence to support the theory that the soul travels to another plane after the body dies.

# 1

# Life After Death: An Overview of Religious Beliefs

## Herbie Brennan

*Herbie Brennan lives in County Carlow, Ireland. He works as a full-time author with an interest in transpersonal psychology, spirituality, comparative religion, reincarnation, esotericism, quantum physics, and psychical research. He has broadcast and lectured widely throughout the United Kingdom and Ireland. He has published more than seventy books, including* Death: The Great Mystery of Life.

Nearly all religions contain teachings about an afterlife. The belief in some sort of life after death has been documented in the early history of most cultures. Each religion has a slightly different view of how the afterlife is attained and what it is like, but most agree that life continues in some form after the body dies.

Ancestor worship has been prevalent throughout the world for tens of thousands of years—so prevalent, indeed, that it still seems to be humanity's most common form of religious expression. Virtually every tribal community on the planet honors its ancestors. There are ancestor shrines in Japan and China. Offerings to the ancestors are made in India (despite widespread belief in reincarnation). A logical corollary to ancestor worship is ancestor survival and the belief that you too will become a helpful ancestor when you die.

The development of urban communities actually enhanced

the concept of an afterlife. Archaeologists have found grave goods in the royal tombs of humankind's earliest civilizations. Close to five thousand years ago, Mesopotamian kings were buried with furniture, musical instruments, and gambling gear for use in the next life. Soldiers and servants were also buried with their masters, apparently to continue their faithful service beyond the grave.

Studies of Sumero-Akkadian mythology indicate a prevalent and widespread belief in an afterlife, although not one you might look forward to with any great enthusiasm. The dead rested—if that is the word—in a realm called *kur-nu-gi-a*, the Land of No Return. They lived in darkness, ate clay, and, according to one myth, were "clothed like birds with wings." When the Goddess Ishtar decided to pay a visit, she threatened the gate-keeper that if he refused to let her in she would smash the door-post and lead the dead up out of their gloomy underworld so they could eat the living. This hint of post-mortem cannibalism reflected common attitudes toward the dead throughout the Fertile Crescent. When you were gone, you might survive, but changed for the worse in an unpleasant environment.

## Ancient ideas of the afterlife

The picture was a lot brighter in Ancient Egypt. Sometime before 2300 B.C., masons cut hieroglyphic texts into the walls of the pyramid of Unas, the last of Egypt's 5th Dynasty Pharaohs. They consisted of prayers, rituals, and magical spells dating to an even earlier time, all designed to guarantee the dead king a comfortable life in the afterworld. Earlier still, Egyptian beliefs postulated a continued existence in the *Sekhet-Aaru* (Field of Reeds) a curious environment possibly based on the Nile marshland inhabited by the primitive hunters of pre-dynastic times.

But the Field of Reeds seems to have been reserved for commoners. Pharaohs, by and large, were supposed to ascend to the heavens and become stars. Later, Egypt became a culture obsessed with death and evolved a complex picture of the human soul. . . .

The concept of an afterlife also emerged in the later civilizations of Greece and Rome. For the early Greeks, life after death was an unedifying existence as an insubstantial shadow inhabiting a gloomy underworld where bloodless shades lacked power and longed for their lost life. This was not Hell (in the common understanding of the term) but rather an eternity of boredom and mediocrity from which only the greatest heroes escaped. Mighty men of renown were believed to avoid death altogether, despite the noticeable fact that most of them met sticky ends on bloody battlefields: they celebrated their victories as immortals in Elysium.

(Much the same theme is seen in the old Norse idea that heroes might sometimes cross the Rainbow Bridge and spend eternity in Valhalla. There they had Odin and his fellow gods for company, fought cheerfully among themselves by day, and joined together for a pork and mead feast by night . . . an idealized vision of a warrior's life if ever there was one.)

> *Egypt became a culture obsessed with death.*

By the sixth century B.C., a more optimistic note had crept into Greek thought with the development of the various mystery religions, initiate groups characterized by secret doctrines and ritual dramas. The Eleusinian Mysteries in particular held out the promise of a blissful afterlife to its members, while the hoi polloi were, as usual, condemned to the same old gloomy underworld.

The Ancient Romans held ideas of an afterlife similar to those of the early Greeks, conceiving of a gloomy shadow realm accessible by means of a one-way boat trip across the River Styx. Ever practical, the Romans realized the ferryman would want payment and placed a coin under the tongue of the corpse for this purpose. The later custom, widespread throughout Europe, of placing coins on the eyes of the dead may be a distorted survival.

## Judaism and the afterlife

Classical Judaism wasn't so sure about an afterlife . . . at least not at first. *Ecclesiastes* (9:5) said it all: "The dead know nothing and they have no more reward." All turned to dust again and a living dog was better than a dead lion. All the same, whatever the official position, belief in some sort of existence after physical death crept in. How else could you explain the story of the Witch of Endor? According to the Old Testament account, the prophet Samuel was dead and buried in Ramah when the Philistine armies threatened Israel. Desperate for advice, King Saul asked a witch to call up the prophet's spirit, which she successfully did.

The appearance of Samuel—whose first words were "Why has thou disquieted me to bring me up?"—suggests his postmortem survival in some realm. That many Israelites believed in such survival is attested by the fact that Saul was forced to ban necromancy in the days before he felt the need of it himself. The practice, it seems, had become widespread throughout his kingdom. . . .

> **Classical Judaism wasn't so sure about an afterlife.**

Sometime in or around the fifth century B.C., an extraordinary development occurred. The Book of Isaiah, a compilation of sayings attributed to the eighth century B.C. prophet of that name, announced that "the dead shall live, their bodies shall rise"—the first recorded example of a belief in physical resurrection. There seems little doubt that physical resurrection is what was meant. Isaiah spoke of corpses as the "dwellers in the dust" and forecast they would "awake and sing."

## Judgment in the afterlife

Physical resurrection soon became linked to the idea of judgment. While the good, the bad and the ugly were all scheduled for a rude awakening, only some would achieve a pleasurable immortality. The rest were condemned to shame and everlasting contempt. . . .

By the time the *Wisdom of Solomon* came to be written during the first century B.C., the idea had emerged that the soul might actually predate the physical body, which it entered at birth. (The same notion had occurred to Plato some centuries earlier.) Although traditional Judaism held firm to earlier teachings, the Pharisees concluded the soul was immortal and fated by the individual's behavior either for damnation or resurrection.

Time passed, but the idea of resurrection simply would not go away. . . .

In the Eighteen Benedictions recited daily, God was addressed as "the One who resurrects the dead" while the Sanhedrin warned that anyone claiming there was no resurrection would be debarred from the world to come. As we shall see, the concept of resurrection was taken up by Christianity, where it remains an article of faith to this day.

## Christianity and the afterlife

Christianity is, in fact, a death-centred religion. Its central focus is the death (and resurrection) of its founder, its central symbol the cross used by the Romans as an instrument of death. It accepts—at least symbolically—the ancient Hebrew idea that Adam and Eve forfeited a natural immortality by their behavior in the Garden of Eden. "The wages of sin is death," thunders *Romans* 6:23. Nonetheless, belief in immortality remains, linked to the concept of salvation through Christ, resurrection of the physical body, and a mass judgment designed to sort out the good, who by definition accept Christ, from the bad, who do not.

Christian ideas about life after death were greatly influenced by a wholly separate doctrine—the Second Coming of Christ. According to the central Christian mythos, Jesus of Nazareth was crucified to death by the Romans but rose from the dead three days later and appeared briefly to some of his disciples before ascending to heaven. As St. Paul told the story, the historical event had a profound spiritual significance. Like those of Osiris and several god-kings before him, Jesus' death was a sacrifice that cleansed humanity of its sins—or at least that portion of humanity who fervently believed it did.

> **// Christianity is, in fact, a death-centered religion. //**

The original expectation was that Jesus, having personally conquered death, would return in glory during the lifetime of his surviving disciples. When the last of them died, the hope was that the return would happen soon, which gradually transformed into confidence that it would happen someday. Since a thousand years seemed like a nice round figure, a millennial belief emerged. There were frissons of popular excitement—not to say outright terror—at the approach of the year A.D. 1000 and again, more recently, the year A.D. 2000. The problem was that Christ's reappearance was supposed to herald a final judgment of everybody everywhere. Fortunately for sinners and the faithless, nothing untoward occurred on either date.

> *❝According to the Qur'an, humans are animated by a vital spirit called* nafs. *❞*

Against this suspenseful background, early Christians became increasingly preoccupied with the question of what happened to the dead while they waited for Christ's return. One theory advanced was that there had to be an immediate individual judgment, an interesting echo of the much earlier Egyptian belief. According to this view, you died, and were judged at once by God and dispatched to heaven or hell according to your just desserts.

## Judgment Day

Although this idea has proven remarkably tenacious—many Christians think in just such terms today—there were those who disagreed with it. An alternative viewpoint was that the dead were in some sense only sleeping as they awaited fulfillment of the prophesied mass resurrection that would mark Judgment Day on a heroic scale.

The idea of a mass Judgment Day had considerable emotional appeal since it tied in nicely with the vision of King Jesus returning in glory to rule our entire planet. But as a theory, it had its problems. One was that it seemed terribly unfair to postpone a true believer's well-earned trip to Paradise, and even more so to postpone the equally well-earned punishments that should surely be meted out by a loving God to sinners at the earliest possible opportunity.

The church father Tertullian bent his considerable intellect to the problem and came up with a solution of sorts. He put forward a "spacial concept"—which he suggested might be called "Abraham's Bosom"—that lay somewhat below heaven but definitely above hell. There the souls of the dead could rest and the just refresh themselves until the final resolution of their fate in a forthcoming Judgment Day. The Byzantine church liked the idea so much that they formally endorsed it as part of Christian doctrine.

The Roman Catholic Church embraced a different version of the idea in the Middle Ages with the introduction of limbo. The term means "border" and limbo was conceived of as existing on the border between heaven and hell. Here souls remained awaiting Judgment Day but with less emphasis on refreshment than in Abraham's Bosom. Long convinced that just about everybody is a sinner, Catholicism suggested penances in limbo might usefully cleanse the soul before the Final Judgment. In the thirteenth century the Church released another interesting detail about the afterlife state. Unbaptized infants, burdened only by original sin, went to hell but were given lighter punishments than the rest of us.

## Islam and the afterlife

The seventh century A.D. saw the beginnings of fresh and highly graphic insights into death with the foundation of Islam by the Prophet Muhammad. According to the Qur'an, humans are animated by a vital spirit called *nafs*, which is the seat of your rational consciousness and associated with your individuality. It is also associated with Allah himself, who "breathed his spirit" into a humanity made from molded mud. This soul is taken away during sleep but returned by God to those destined to survive the night.

> *Virtually every culture in the Western world has harbored beliefs about an afterlife.*

On death, the soul rises to the throat before leaving the body altogether, then meets with *Malak al-Mawt*, the Angel of Death, who instructs the wicked to depart to the wrath of God. Many nervously attempt to disobey the order and seek refuge back in the body from whence they have to be extricated "like the dragging of an iron skewer through moist wool." Once evicted out in this way, the soul is placed by angels in a malodorous hair cloth and its sins carefully recorded before it is returned to the corpse in the grave.

The righteous have it altogether easier. They are told by the Angel of Death to depart to the mercy of God and flow gracefully from the body to be wrapped by angels in a perfumed shroud and taken to the Seventh Heaven, where their virtues are recorded. But these souls too are returned to the body in the grave.

At this point, the *Fitnat al-Qabr* begins. This graveside trial is conducted by two angels, Munkar and Nakir, who question the deceased about the tenets of Islam. Those who fail the test discover that their tomb contracts violently, crushing them so that their ribs pile up on top of one another. A mystical door opens and the smoke and heat of hell pours in. By contrast, those who pass the test have their graves expanded as far as the eye can see. But this state of affairs is temporary in both cases. After a period known as *al-barzakh*, good and bad alike are resurrected in physical bodies to face *Yaum al-Hisab*, the Final Judgment. This sends believers to well-stocked "gardens in which rivers flow" where they will abide forever, while the wicked are condemned to hell, where they don garments of fire and have boiling water poured over their heads. New skin is substituted for the old that burns away so the damned can continue to feel their punishment.

Islamic martyrs are excused from the judgment process altogether. Those killed in a holy war or who suffered harm in the defense of their beliefs are forgiven any sins they might have committed and are sent directly to the paradise gardens. . . .

What are we to make of all this? It is clear that virtually every culture in the Western world has harbored beliefs about an afterlife. In earliest times, these seem to have been confined to an immaterial existence in some sort of alternative dimension, but later the idea of immortality in a specially resurrected (physical) body became widespread.

# 2

# Christian Beliefs About Life After Death

## Patrick Zukeran

*Patrick Zukeran is an associate speaker for Probe Ministries. He has a BA in religion from Point Loma Nazarene University and an MA in theology from Dallas Theological Seminary. He is an author, radio talk show host, and a national and international speaker on apologetics, cults, world religions, the Bible, theology, and current issues.*

Christians believe that there is life after death. Although phenomena such as near death experiences suggest that at death the soul separates from the body, it is the writings of the Bible that are the basis of Christian belief in life after death. After death, devout Christians are united with their god in heaven, where they are reunited with loved ones who have died before them. Unbelievers are judged and sentenced to hell.

## Differing perspectives on death

For the entire existence of mankind, we have struggled with the question, "What happens after death?" Our answer to this dilemma has great implications for our life here on earth. Although many avoid the issue, we must sooner or later address the question. There are many competing answers to this question.

Atheists believe that at death one ceases to exist. There is no afterlife or eternal soul that continues in eternity. All there is to look forward to is our inevitable death, the future death of mankind, and the universe. It is in the face of this future that the athe-

Patrick Zukeran, "What Happens After Death?" www.probe.org, November 19, 2003. Copyright © 2003 by Patrick Zukeran. Reproduced by permission.

ist must seek to find meaning and purpose for his own existence.

The Eastern and New Age religions that hold to a pantheistic worldview teach that one goes through an endless cycle of reincarnation until the cycle is broken and the person becomes one with the divine. What form a person becomes in the next life depends on the quality of life lived in the previous life. When one unites with the divine, he ceases to exist as an individual, but becomes part of the divine life force, like a drop of water returning to the ocean.

Those who hold to the animistic or tribal religions believe that after death the human soul remains on the earth or travels to join the departed spirits of the ancestors in the underworld, also called the realm of the shadows. For eternity they wander in darkness, experiencing neither joy nor sorrow. Some of the spirits of the deceased may be called upon to aid or torment those on earth.

Islam teaches that at the end of history, God will judge the works of all men. Those whose good deeds outweigh their bad deeds will enter into paradise. The rest will be consigned to hell. The Koran teaches that in paradise men will be drinking wine and entertained by heavenly maidens and that they may take several of these maidens for their wives.

Most worldviews must accept their belief in the afterlife on *untested* faith, but the Christian hope is sure for two reasons; the resurrection of Christ and the testimony of God's Word. The Bible gives us the true view of what happens after death. However, many Christians have a misunderstanding of the afterlife. Some believe that they become one of the angels, others believe they go into a state of "soul sleep," while others believe they will be floating on clouds playing harps. . . .

Christians can be assured that death is not something to be feared. Instead, at death we arrive home in heaven. To live means we exist in a foreign country. Death has lost its sting and now is a victory through the resurrection of Jesus our Lord.

## Near death experiences

For the past thirty years, thousands of people have reported experiencing what are called near death experiences (NDEs). NDEs are encounters where a person, being in full awareness, leaves the body and enters another world. Such experiences have resulted in life transformation in many individuals. What are we to make of these accounts?

Let us understand that NDEs come from those who have been *clinically* dead, not *biologically* dead. In clinical death, external life signs such as consciousness, pulse, and breathing cease. In such cases, biological death results if no steps are taken to reverse the process. Biological death, on the other hand, is not affected by any amount of attention, for it is physically irreversible.

The NDE accounts occur at various stages of clinical death. Some occur when the patient is comatose, very close to death, or pronounced clinically dead. Other accounts occur when the patient's heart stops beating. Others occur while the patient's brain ceases to register any activity on the EEG monitor. There have not been any cases of biological or irreversible death for a significant amount of time followed by a resurrection.

What has intrigued scientists and theologians in their study of NDEs is that many of the patients have similar experiences. These include leaving the body and watching from above as doctors work on it, entering a dark tunnel, seeing light, seeing others, meeting a spirit being, experiencing peace, and then returning to the body.

Scientists and doctors from various worldviews have sought to explain this phenomenon. Those from an atheistic worldview have sought to give naturalistic explanations. Their explanations range from hallucination induced by medication, chemical reactions the brain experiences in near death crises, previous encounters long forgotten, and others. These fall short of explaining NDE events. . . .

NDEs may not conclusively prove there is a heaven or hell, but they do indicate that at death the soul separates from the body, and that a person's spirit is conscious and coherent at death.

However, NDEs do not accurately reflect what lies beyond the grave. NDEs deal with accounts that give a short glimpse behind the curtain of death and therefore they give us an incomplete picture. . . .

## Can we communicate with the dead?

Do the spirits of the dead have the ability to communicate with the living? One of the most popular current TV shows is "Crossing Over," with psychic John Edward. He, like other psychics, claims to have the ability to communicate with the spirits of the deceased. He amazes spectators with his ability to reveal details about which only the deceased loved one may have known. From this communication, people attempt to receive comfort, advice, and encouragement.

The Bible teaches that communication with the dead is not possible. Throughout the Bible God commands His people not to indulge in the practice of necromancy, the art of communicating with the dead. . . .

> *The Bible gives us the true view of what happens after death.*

The Canaanites consulted spirits and the dead in hopes of gaining power and predicting future events. This practice is an abomination to God and it is for this reason the Canaanites were ejected from the land. Israel was warned not to imitate the Canaanites or they too would suffer a similar fate.

Contacting the dead is forbidden because the spirits of the dead cannot contact the living. In Luke 16, the rich man who was suffering in hell sought a way to communicate with his living family to warn them of their fate. However, he was not able to communicate in any way nor could the living communicate with him.

Who, then, are mediums and spiritists contacting? If they are indeed contacting a spiritual being, it is most likely a demonic counterfeit. Although the demonic spirit may communicate some truths, the ultimate intention of the spirit is to deceive and take one away from the Lord. This practice can ultimately lead to demonic possession and injury to the person. . . .

## One minute after death

What happens when we breathe our final breath? The Bible teaches what will occur.

First our immaterial soul and spirit will be separated from our physical body. Second, we will immediately receive the judgment that will determine our eternal destiny. Those who have trusted in Christ's payment on the cross for our sins will enter into eternal life in the presence of God. . . .

Those who reject this gift, will receive what they have chosen, eternity separated from God in Hell. Hebrews 9:27 states,

"Just as man is destined to die once, and after that to face judgment." There is no second chance and there is no cycle of reincarnation. Our eternal destiny is determined by the decision we make for Christ here on earth.

Many assume that after receiving Christ all that remains is a joyful entrance into heaven. Scripture teaches that Jesus will reward us according to how we lived our life on earth. He taught this principle in the parable of the talents in Luke 19. Each servant was entrusted to administer the talents the master gave him. Upon the return of the master, each servant had to give an account for his stewardship. The wise servants were rewarded doubly while the wicked servant was removed.

> *Christians can be assured that death is not something to be feared.*

The lesson for the Christian is that each of us will give an account for our time here on earth. This is not the same as being judged on our salvation status. Christ's death on the cross allows all who believe to enter God's kingdom. We will be judged on our works done since the time of our salvation. This judgment of believers is called the *Bema Seat judgment*. This event is described in 1 Corinthians 3:11–15:

> For no man can lay a foundation other than the one which is laid, which is Jesus Christ. Now if any man builds upon the foundation with gold, silver, precious stones, wood, hay or straw, each man's work will become evident; for the day will show it, because it is to be revealed with fire; and the fire itself will test the quality of each man's work. If any man's work, which he has built upon it, remains, he shall receive a reward. If any man's work is burned up, he shall suffer loss; but he himself shall be saved, yet so as through fire. . . .

At the Bema Seat, our works will be tested with divine fire. Those works that were done for the glory of God will endure the flames and will be our reward. Some will regretfully see all their works on earth burned up before their eyes and enter heaven with little or no reward.

The unbeliever will be judged and sentenced to hell. At the end of the age, he faces the Great White Throne judgment. Here, all the unrighteous dead from the beginning of time are judged based on their rejection of the Savior. They are then thrown into the lake of fire for eternity. Revelation 20:11–15 says:

> And I saw a great white throne and Him who sat upon it, from whose presence earth and heaven fled away, and no place was found for them. And I saw the dead, the great and the small, standing before the throne, and the books were opened; . . . and the dead were judged from the things which were written in the books, according to their deeds. . . . And if anyone's name was not found written in the book of life, he was thrown into the lake of fire.

Knowing that as Christians we will one day give an account for our lives, we should live as wise stewards over what God has given us. Knowing the fate of the unsaved should fill us with boldness to share Christ unashamedly, with urgency to all. Knowing what lies beyond the grave should motivate us to live life on earth with a mission. . . .

## What will we do in heaven?

What will we do in heaven for all eternity? Some envision playing golf for eternity, while others envision saints floating on clouds strumming harps of gold. Although great thoughts, they fall short of the glorious future that actually awaits those in Christ. We are told relatively little about what activities will occur in heaven. We are only given a brief glimpse of our life to come.

> *NDEs do not accurately reflect what lies beyond the grave.*

First, the moment that saints of all the ages anticipate is seeing the Lord they served face to face. This will be the first and greatest moment after physical death. From then on we will have fellowship in His presence for all eternity.

Second, our life in heaven involves worship. A vivid picture is found in Revelation 19:1–5:

> After this I heard what seemed to be the mighty
> voice of a great multitude in heaven, crying, "Hal-
> lelujah! Salvation and glory and power belong to
> our God, for true and just are his judgments. . . ."
> And again they shouted, "Hallelujah! The smoke
> from her goes up for ever and ever." And the
> twenty-four elders and the four living creatures fell
> down and worshipped God who was seated on the
> throne, saying, "Amen. Hallelujah." Then a voice
> came from the throne saying: "Praise our God, all
> you his servants, you who fear him both small and
> great."

Like the sound of roaring waters comes the praise from the saints of all ages. Recently the men from our church described the experience of singing the hymn How Great Thou Art at a Promise Keepers [men's Christian group] conference. Nothing they said could accurately describe that majestic experience. The closest they could come to putting it into words was, "Awesome! Just awesome!" Can you imagine what it will be like when we sing "Holy, Holy, Holy" along with the saints of all ages in the presence of God? Our worship here is preparation for our future, grand worship in heaven.

> *What awaits the believer after death is a glorious future that cannot truly be imagined!*

Third is the aspect of rest. Heavenly rest here does not mean a cessation from activity, but the experience of reaching a goal of crucial importance. In Hebrews 4:9–11 the writer, addressing the people of God states, "There remains, then, a Sabbath rest for the people of God; for anyone who enters God's rest also rests from his own work, just as God did from his." Heaven is the final goal reached after our pilgrimage here on earth. We will rest from our sufferings and struggles against sickness, the flesh, the world, and the devil.

Fourth, we will serve the Lord. Luke 19:11–27 teaches a parable about stewardship. The wise servants who multiplied their master's talents were given rule over ten and five cities. Revelation 22:3 tells us, "The throne of God and of the Lamb will be in the city and his servants will serve him." In 1 Corinthians 6:3 Paul rebukes the carnal Christians who cannot settle their own disputes and asks them, "Do you not know that we will judge angels?" In Revelation 3:21 the Lord Jesus promises, "To him who overcomes, I will give the right to sit with Me on my throne, just as I overcame and sat down with my Father on His throne." Apparently we will be given authority over a sphere in God's eternal kingdom. How much we are given depends on our faithfulness to Him on this earth.

Fifth, we will experience fellowship with God and with one another. One of the most painful experiences in life is to say goodbye. Whether it is to see loved ones move to another residence or because of death, farewells are a painful time. For the Christian, there is hope in knowing, our goodbyes are not permanent. One day we will meet again and this time we will never say goodbye again. What awaits the believer after death is a glorious future that cannot truly be imagined!

# 3

# Islamic Beliefs About Life After Death

## Hadhrat Mirza Tahir Ahmad

*Hadhrat Mirza Tahir Ahmad was born in 1928 in Qadian, India. He was educated in India, Pakistan, and in the United Kingdom. In 1982 he was elected as the head of the international Ahmadiyya Muslim Community, which he served until his death in 2003. He is the author of many books, including* An Elementary Study of Islam.

The Islamic view of the afterlife is very different from the Christian view. Some Islamics view heaven as a paradise much like earth, but many believe that heaven and hell are indescribable and beyond the realm of human understanding. They also believe that heaven and hell are not two different places but that they coexist without interrelating. Each individual creates a heaven or hell according to his or her spiritual state—a healthy soul experiences the nearness of God while an unhealthy one feels tormented.

The question of life after death has always agitated the minds of people belonging to all religions and all ages alike. There is also the atheistic view which totally denies the possibility of life after death. The religions which believe in life after death can be divided into two categories.

1. Those which believe in the reincarnation of the soul of a dead person into a new human or animal form of existence.

2. Those which believe in an otherworldly state of existence after death. The atheistic view is outside the domain of this discussion. As far as Islamic doctrine is concerned, Islam

Hadhrat Mirza Tahir Ahmad, *An Elementary Study of Islam*. Tilford, UK: Islam International Publications, Ltd., 1996. ISBN: 1 85372 562 5. All rights reserved. Reproduced by permission.

belongs to that category of religions which totally rejects all possibilities of reincarnation in any form. But those who believe in some otherworldly form of spiritual or carnal existence are divided among themselves on so many planes. Within each religion the understanding differs. Hence, with reference to the views held by the followers of various religions, no belief can be attributed to them without fear of contradiction.

## Two views of heaven

In Islam itself there are different views held by different sects of Muslim scholars. The general understanding tends to perceive the otherworldly form as very similar to the carnal one here on earth. The concept of heaven and hell consequently present a material image rather than a spiritual image of things to be. Heaven is presented, according to their concept, as an immeasurably large garden literally abounding in beautiful trees casting eternal shadows under which rivers will flow. The rivers would be of milk and honey. The garden will be fruit bearing and all man may desire of fruits would be his at his command. The meat would be that of birds of all sorts; it is only for one to wish which meat he particularly craves. Female companions of exceeding beauty and refinement would be provided to the pious men, with no limit imposed on the number, which will be decided according to their capacity. As many as they can cope with will be theirs. What would they do? How would they relate with each other? Will they bear children or lead a barren life of enjoyment? These are all the mute questions. The enjoyment, as it is conceived, is intensely sensual. No work to be performed, no labour to be wasted, no effort to be made. A perfect life (if such life can be called perfect) of complete and total indolence, with the option of overeating and over-drinking, because also wine will be flowing close to the rivers of milk and honey. No fear of dyspepsia or intoxication! Reclining on heavenly cushions of silk and brocade, they will while their time away in eternal bliss—but what an eternal bliss!

In Islam, there are others who categorically reject this naive understanding of the Quranic references to heaven, and prove with many a reference to verses of the Holy Quran that what it describes is just metaphorical imagery which has no carnality about it. In fact the Holy Quran makes it amply clear that the form of existence of the life to come will be so different from all known forms of life here on earth, that it is beyond human imagination even to have the slightest glimpse of the other-worldly realities.

> We will raise you into a form of which you have not the slightest knowledge. *Surah Al-Waqiah (Ch. 56.: V.62)*

This [statement above] is the categorical statement of the Quran on the subject. In recent times, the founder of the Ahmadiyya Community, Hadrat Mirza Ghulam Ahmad of Qadian, presented this view of spiritual existence as against carnal existence in his unique and outstanding treatise entitled *The Philosophy of the Teachings of Islam*. All views propounded in the book are well documented with Quranic references and traditions of the Holy Founder of Islam. A brief account is reproduced here.

> *The concept of hell and heaven in Islam is completely different from the normally held view.*

According to his profound study, the life in the hereafter would not be material. Instead, it would be of a spiritual nature of which we can only visualise certain aspects. We cannot determine precisely how things will take shape. One of the salient features of his vision of the hereafter concerns the soul giving birth to another rarer entity, which would occupy the same position in relation to the soul as the soul occupies in relation to our carnal existence here on earth. This birth of a soul from within the soul will be related to the sort of life that we have lived here on earth. If our lives here are spent in submission to the will of God and in accordance with His commands, our tastes gradually become cultured and attuned to enjoying spiritual pleasures as against carnal pleasures. Within the soul a sort of embryonic soul begins to take shape. New faculties are born and new tastes are acquired, in which those accustomed to carnal pleasures find no enjoyment. These new types of refined human beings can find the content of their heart. Sacrifice instead of the usurpation of others' rights becomes enjoyable. Forgiveness takes the upper hand of revenge, and love with no selfish motive is born like a second nature, replacing all relationships that have ulterior motives. Thus, one can say a new soul within the soul is in the offing.

> **"** *Each individual creates his own hell or his own heaven.* **"**

All these projections regarding the development of the soul are inferences drawn from various verses of the Holy Quran, yet the exact nature of future events cannot be precisely determined. One can only say that something along these lines would take place, the details of which lie beyond the reach of human understanding. There are certain aspects of the new life which need to be discussed. The concept of hell and heaven in Islam is completely different from the normally held view. Hell and heaven are not two different places occupying separate time and space. According to the Holy Quran, the heaven covers the entire universe. 'Where would be hell then?' enquired some of the companions of the Holy Prophet. 'At the same place', was the answer, 'but you do not have the faculty to understand their coexistence.' That is to say in ordinary human terms, they may seem to occupy the same time-space, but in reality because they belong to different dimensions, so they will coexist without interfering and inter-relating with each other.

## A personalized heaven and hell

But what is the meaning of heavenly bliss, the tortures of the fire of hell? In answer to this question, the Promised Messiah has illustrated the issue in the following terms: If a man is almost dying of thirst, and is otherwise healthy, cool water can provide him such deeply satisfying pleasure as cannot be derived from the ordinary experience of drinking water, or even the most delicious drink of his choice. If a man is thirsty and hungry as well, and he needs an immediate source of energy, a chilled bunch of grapes can provide him with such deep satisfaction as is not experienced by the same in ordinary circumstances. But the pre-requisite for these pleasures is good health. Now visualise a very sick man, who is nauseating and trying to vomit whatever liquid is left in him, and is at the verge of death through dehydration. Offer him a glass of cool water, or a chilled bunch of grapes, then not to mention his accepting them, a mere glance of them would create a state of revulsion and absolute abhorrence in him.

In illustrations like these, the Promised Messiah made it clear that hell and heaven are only issues of relativity. A healthy soul which has acquired the taste for good things, when brought into close proximity of the objects of its choice, will draw even greater pleasure than before. All that a healthy spiritual man was craving was nearness to God and His attributes and to imitate divine virtues. In heaven, such a healthy soul would begin to see and conceive and feel the nearness of the attributes of God like never before. They, according to the Promised Messiah, would not remain merely spiritual values, but would acquire ethereal forms and shapes, which the newly born heavenly spirit would enjoy with the help of the erstwhile soul, which would function as the body. That again would be a matter of relativity. The converse will be true of hell, in the sense that an unhealthy soul would create an unhealthy body for the new soul of the hereafter. And the same factors which provide pleasure to the healthy soul would provide torture and deep suffering for this unhealthy entity. . . .

> *Spiritual life will progress gradually through many stages.*

In short, each individual creates his own hell or his own heaven, and in accordance with his own state each heaven differs from the other person's heaven, and each hell differs from the other person's hell, though apparently they occupy the same space and time in otherworldly dimensions.

## Transformation of the soul

What happens to man's soul between the time of his carnal death and his resurrection on the Day of Judgement? The Holy Prophet is reported to have said that after our death windows will open up in the grave; for the pious people, windows open from heaven, and for the wicked people they open towards hell. However, if we were to open up a grave, we would not find any windows! So literal acceptance of these words will not convey the true meaning of this subject. It is impossible that the Holy Prophet should ever misinform us, hence here he had to be speaking metaphorically. Had it not been so, then every time we dig up a grave, we should find windows, either opening into hell, or letting in the fragrant and pleasant air of paradise. But we witness neither of these. So what do the Holy Prophet's words mean?

> *Man's resurrection is described as a transformation that he cannot envisage.*

The grave is actually an intermediary phase of existence between this life and the life to come. Here, spiritual life will progress gradually through many stages until it reaches its ultimate destiny. Then by the Command of Allah, a trumpet will be blown, and the final spiritual form will come into being. In this interim period, different souls would pass through a semblance of heaven or hell before reaching their final stage of perfection, fit and ready to be raised into a completely transformed entity. . . .

## How long does transformation take?

The question that now arises is: Will the soul also progress as does the child in the mother's womb, and will it pass through all these stages? The answer to this can be found in . . . the Quran: '*Ma khalakakum wa ma basukum illa ka nafsin wahidin*'— your first creation and your second creation will be identical.

To understand the second creation, we need to understand the way a baby takes shape in a mother's womb. These forms apparently only take nine months to develop, while in reality the creation of life is spread over billions of years. Going back to the beginning of zoological life, the baby passes through almost all the stages of the evolution of life. From the beginning of the pregnancy, through to its culmination nine months later, the development of the child reflects all the stages of creation. In other words, all the phases of evolution are being repeated in those nine months, one after the other, and at such great speed that it is beyond our imagination. It keeps alive the stages of the system of evolution, and presents a picture of it.

The creation of life underwent a long period of development to reach the form that we witness in nine months. This sheds light on the fact that the period of our first creation was very long, and our second creation will also span a long period. By studying these nine months we can learn something of the billions of years of the history of life, and also about the evolution of souls in the next world. It is perhaps safe to infer that the time from the early origin of life to the ultimate creation of man, would perhaps be needed once again for the development of the soul after the death.

In support of this reasoning, the Quran categorically declares that when the souls are resurrected they will talk to one another, trying to determine how long they tarried on the earth. Some will say, 'We tarried for a day' while others will say 'for even less than a day.' Allah will then say: 'No even that is not correct.' In other words, Allah will say that 'You tarried on earth for much less than what you estimate.' In reality, the relationship of one life-span to a small part of the day is more or less the same ratio that the time of the soul's resurrection will have to its previous entire life. The further away something is, the smaller it appears. Our childhood seems like an experience of just a few seconds. The greater the distance of the stars, the smaller they appear. What Allah is trying to tell us is that we won't find ourselves being judged the very next day after we die. Instead, judgement will take place in such a distant future that our previous lives will seem like a matter of a few seconds to us, like a small point a long way away.

In short, man's resurrection is described as a transformation that he cannot envisage and an event that is as certain as his existence here on earth. All these subjects have been explained in detail in the Holy Quran.

# 4

# Science Suggests There Is an Afterlife

## Jeffery L. Sheler

*Jeffery L. Sheler is an award-winning journalist and has written about religion for* U.S. News & World Report *for nine years. He is a correspondent for the PBS television program* Religion & Ethics Newsweekly. *Sheler is also the author of* Is the Bible True?

Since ancient times, Christians and Jews have believed in the concept of heaven. Even in today's scientific era, nearly 80 percent of Americans of various faiths believe in an afterlife despite a lack of proof. Some might wonder how educated, modern people can adhere to such seemingly outmoded beliefs. However, scientists have become increasingly open to the idea that there is a grand design to the universe that includes the possibility of life after death. Scientists and theologians are now exchanging views on many issues.

Easter at its essence is about a belief in the triumph of life over death. It is one faith's response to the mystery that has haunted humankind since our first contemplative ancestors gazed into the abyss of death and trembled. What, if anything, awaits beyond the grave?

As Christians celebrate the Resurrection this holy season, they will affirm their faith that Jesus Christ arose from the dead and, in doing so, made "life everlasting" a possibility for all. "We are born," says Andrew Greeley, a Roman Catholic priest and University of Chicago sociologist, "with two incurable diseases: life, from which we die, and hope, which says maybe death isn't the end." To hope for life in the hereafter is a part of human nature.

All of this will strike some—as it did [psychologist] Sigmund Freud, [Communist leader] Karl Marx, and other noted critics of religion—as wishful, largely superstitious thinking that does little more than sap human creativity and divert attention from earthly misery. It is easy to dismiss belief in the afterlife as a relic of ancient cultures that believed in a celestial city above the clouds and a fiery subterranean hell.

But to many modern believers, those old ideas are still vital, even if less vivid. While the notion of life after death has roots in ancient Greek philosophy and corollaries in other religions, the primary window on the afterlife for many Christians and Jews remains the Bible. The scriptures present an evolving picture with few concrete details, giving believers broad imaginative license. . . .

## The concept of heaven

The Old Testament portrays heaven as a celestial sphere "above the vault of the earth" from which God, surrounded by his angels, rules his creation. But there is no suggestion in the most ancient Hebrew texts that heaven is the final repository of human souls. Throughout most of the Old Testament, deceased humans, good and evil, were said to end up in Sheol, a gloomy netherworld separated from God, much like the Hades of Greek mythology. Only in later Judaism did belief in a final resurrection of the dead and a heavenly "world to come" appear.

> *It is easy to dismiss belief in the afterlife as a relic of ancient cultures.*

In the New Testament, Jesus spoke of the "kingdom of heaven" as a place of eternal reward with "many dwelling places." He tells his followers in the Gospel According to John:

I go to prepare a place for you, and if I go to prepare a place for you I will come again, and receive you to myself; that where I am there you may be also.

The apostle Paul assured believers that a "house not made with hands, eternal in the heavens," awaited them. Writing to

Christians in Corinth, Paul even refers to his own mystical journey into "the third heaven" where he "heard inexpressible words, which a man is not permitted to speak." But he gives no visual description of the heavenly landscape.

The most vivid and familiar biblical images of heaven appear in the apocalyptic book of Revelation. It is there, in the mystical vision of a prophet named John, that we find the often popularized descriptions of pearly gates and streets of gold, of a vast white throne, and of throngs of saints and angels gathered around God at the culmination of history. But the meaning and significance of those images are widely debated and often misunderstood. The picture of the end times in the book of Revelation, says N.T. Wright, dean of the Anglican cathedral in Lichfield, Staffordshire, England, "isn't about humans being snatched up from earth to heaven." Rather, he writes in a recent issue of the *Christian Century*, "the holy city, new Jerusalem, comes down from heaven to earth. God's space and ours are finally married, integrated at last." That, says Wright, is what Christians pray for when they say "thy kingdom come" in the Lord's Prayer.

> **❝ *Dialogue between scientists and theologians has become increasingly common.* ❞**

Christian theologians traditionally have viewed Revelation as a glimpse not just into heaven but into future events, Judgment Day, and the end of the present world. Some scholars, on the other hand, contend it is more properly understood as "resistance literature" intended to exhort first-century Christians living in Asia Minor to "stand firm in the faith" against the threat of Roman persecution. Even so, the evocative imagery of Revelation continues to have a powerful influence on Christian views of the afterlife.

Should believers expect to see alabaster houses and gold-paved streets in heaven? Biblical scholars treat those images as vibrantly metaphorical. They illustrate what theologians regard as perhaps most important to understand about the Judeo-Christian concept of heaven: It means dwelling forever in the presence of God. Without the specific imagery of houses and gates and city streets, says Martin Marty, a University of Chicago religion historian, "we have no way of imagining what it's like being with God" in the hereafter.

## Scientific faith

Strikingly, nearly 80 percent of Americans—of various religious faiths and of none—say they believe in life after death, and two thirds are certain there is a heaven. This may be explained by the religious nature of society today. By almost every measure, the United States is a nation steeped in religion, more so than all other Western nations except Poland and Ireland.

Yet this religious pitch occurs in an epoch of science. We can understand the anguished hope of those among us who, in the midst of pain, grief, or oppression, find solace in anticipating a better shake in the next life. But in an age of cloning and quantum physics, of supercomputers and the Hubble Space Telescope, some might reasonably wonder how "normal," educated people can cling to such archaic beliefs.

Despite the apparent contradiction, during the past half century science has moved from a dogmatic denial of realities beyond its reach toward an appreciation of their possibility. Dialogue between scientists and theologians has become increasingly common. Dozens of organizations worldwide now provide forums for exchanges of religious and scientific views on issues ranging from cosmology to the environment. From Albert Einstein to Stephen Hawking, scientists have grown more comfortable in using the word "God" in pondering questions of meaning and order.

> *We are no longer forced to choose between believing either that heaven is a city in the sky somewhere or that it doesn't exist at all.*

New scientific revelations about supernovas, black holes, quarks, and the big bang even suggest to some scientists that there is a "grand design" in the universe—an argument that theologians like Augustine and Thomas Aquinas advanced centuries ago. The presence of intelligent, self-aware beings in the universe, writes Australian physicist Paul Davies in his 1992 book, *The Mind of God*, "can be no trivial detail, no minor by-product of mindless, purposeless forces. We are truly meant to be here." Were scientists to discover a long-sought "theory of everything" to explain the workings of the varying mechanisms of the universe, wrote Hawking in his 1988 book, *A Brief History of Time*, "we would truly know the mind of God."

Perhaps as important, modern science has provided a new language and a new set of symbols for believers to more easily imagine God and eternity. Einstein's theory of relativity, which challenged the Newtonian view of absolute time operating everywhere in the universe, suddenly added a new level of meaning to the biblical injunction that "with the Lord, one day is as a thousand years."

## Science and the afterlife

Speculation in science about such things as parallel universes, new dimensions, and anomalies in the time-space continuum, even if not fully understood by laymen, has provided a conceptual framework for thinking about heaven and post-mortem existence in ways that were not available 100 or even 50 years ago. "We are no longer forced to choose between believing either that heaven is a city in the sky somewhere or that it doesn't exist at all," explains Richard McBrien, a theology professor at the University of Notre Dame. "Now we can think of heaven as an alternate state, perhaps as another dimension." While such imagery is unlikely to foster belief where none exists, says McBrien, "it expands the options for those who are at least open to the possibility" of life after death.

In a society where science and religion flourish side by side, then, remaining open to the idea of the afterlife seems a reasonable posture. Science can't prove the existence of heaven, but its findings have made it easier for some people to believe. While the Christian creed asks adherents to affirm "life everlasting," it requires no assent to the speculative details. It's possible to adhere to the "hope of heaven" and be agnostic about the particulars.

In his book *Teaching Your Children About God*, Rabbi David Wolpe, a professor at the Jewish Theological Seminary of America, recalls an ancient Jewish parable about twin fetuses lying together in the womb. One believes that there is a world beyond the womb, "where people walk upright, where there are mountains and oceans, a sky filled with stars. The other can barely contain his contempt for such foolish ideas."

Suddenly the "believer" is forced through the birth canal leaving behind the only way of life he has known. The remaining fetus is saddened, convinced that a great catastrophe has befallen his companion. "Outside the womb, however, the parents are rejoicing. For what the remaining brother, left behind, has just witnessed is not death but birth." This, Wolpe reminds us, is a classic view of the afterlife—a birth into a world that we on earth can only try to imagine.

# 5

# Science Cannot Prove There Is an Afterlife

## David L. Edwards

*David L. Edwards retired in 1994 as provost of Southwalk Cathedral in England. He was formerly a fellow at All Souls College at Oxford, an editor at SCM Press, subdean of Westminster Abbey, and speaker's chaplain in the House of Commons. Edwards is the author of several books, including* After Death? Past Beliefs and Real Possibilities.

Many cultures have long believed in life after death. The desire for scientific proof of its existence has grown as science has developed and unraveled many of life's mysteries. Research of peoples' near death experiences have found some evidence to support a belief in the afterlife. However, ultimately the existence of an afterlife cannot be proved by science.

In the modern era, dominated by the sciences and their practical applications in technology, some have thought that the ancient question about life after death ought not to be left to the makers of myths, to the teachers of religion, to the philosophers or to the poets. Nor should the answers be given in the form of mere beliefs. . . . Anecdotes galore have circulated in all the centuries and all the continents about encounters with the paranormal. But in modern times the age-old wonder has been turned into research which uses methods not completely unlike an investigation into the possibility of life on the moon or Mars. A cold, hard knife has been inserted into 'pie in the sky when you die'.

This modern concentration has been on experiences re-

David L. Edwards, *After Death? Past Beliefs and Real Possibilities*. London: Cassell, 1999. Copyright © 1999 by David L. Edwards. All rights reserved. Reproduced by permission.

ceived physically, tested for their authenticity by scientific methods and if possible repeated under the controls which are standard in professionally recognized laboratories. It is thought that if human beings have 'minds' or 'spirits' which do not entirely depend on the possession of material bodies, and which are therefore capable of surviving death, it ought to be possible to prove this by experiences which are undeniably authentic encounters with reality. Such findings could be incorporated into the normal scientific world-view and it would become more easily credible that disembodied spirits could exist and could communicate with each other and with us even if 'dead'. Or so it has been hoped. And the hope remains at the end of the twentieth century. . . .

## Speaking with the dead

So what have been the results of this modern search? Emanuel Swedenborg, a Swedish scientist and engineer who died in 1772, was the most famous of the pioneers who claimed to be able to describe the conditions of the dead from direct experience. He published many accounts of visions which he said were reports of visits to another world, inhabited by the angels who taught the dead how to develop their own higher natures. People who refused to learn were sent off to hell but otherwise this world of the dead was not alarming, for here everything physical (including marriage) had an improved version which was spiritual, and in the background God presided benevolently. The dead took a kindly and active interest in the affairs of the living; for example, Swedenborg was instructed how to guide an enquirer to a hidden will which was advantageous. Some Swedenborgian churches have survived—and Swedenborg's picture of another world has also survived, at least in outline.

> *The dead took a kindly and active interest in the affairs of the living.*

Around the middle of the next century, interest intensified in claims that spirits without bodies, including spirits of the dead, could communicate with the living. Spiritualism began

in the excitement produced by claims that noises and distur-
bances caused by spirits had been experienced in the USA. . . .
As the decline of traditional religious beliefs in the West dis-
turbed many, curiosity about the claims of spiritualists also became widespread. The curiosity could produce scepticism. Many
'mediums' or 'sensitives' who purported to hear and convey
messages from the dead, often through raps on a table or 'spirit
writing', were proved to be frauds, and questions were asked
about those who were sincere: did they hypnotize themselves or
others into believing that they were really in touch with the
dead and did they display a surprisingly accurate knowledge
about the living people around them because they had used
telepathy to 'read their minds'? But the feeling was widespread
that 'there may be something in it'.

Serious interest in these new developments led to the for-
mation of the Society for Psychical Research in London in
1882. The founders included not only literary figures but also
distinguished scientists and philosophers. Their initiative was
copied in many other countries. (In France, for example, the
most popular writer about science in the second half of the
century, Camille Flammarion, was fascinated by spiritualism.
So was the philosopher Henri Bergson.) The intention was to
encourage investigations into 'those faculties of Man, real or
supposed, which appear to be inexplicable on any generally
recognized hypothesis'.

> **❝** *Ghost stories could be said to have begun in the imagination.* **❞**

The most secure discovery was that considerable numbers
of people were convinced that they had seen or felt 'apparitions' of the dead, particularly of relatives or friends who were
dying or recently dead, including some who had moved many
miles away or whose critical condition was for other reasons
unknown to the recipients. These reports suggested something
akin to an outburst of psychical energy in some of the dying,
an outburst able to cross the frontiers erected by what scientists
knew as natural laws. That was startling. But these reports
seemed to be in a category different from the stories about
ghosts which had circulated in every human society around

the world. Ghost stories could be said to have begun in the imagination interpreting ordinary noises or lights, or in the desire to impress, and anyway they usually reported appearances which did not fit into people's feelings about what was 'right'. They almost always occurred by night when the reasoning powers of the living were at a low level, and in distressing circumstances such as burial grounds or places where the dead had been very unhappy. If the ghosts spoke it was almost always with complaints (about not being avenged, or not being buried properly, or not being fed after death, to give three examples) and with messages of doom and gloom. Conceivably, ghosts had somehow left behind lasting traces of their misery (before suicide, for example), but they were far less welcome than the dearly loved relatives or friends now widely believed to have made their survival, and often also their happiness, known to some of the living whom they loved. Interest in the possibility of receiving such assurance grew naturally during and after the heavy casualties in the First World War. 'We want a religion you can prove' declared Sir Arthur Conan Doyle, the creator of Sherlock Holmes and an enthusiast for investigations of the 'spirit world' much in the style used so brilliantly by that detective. A leading scientist, Sir Oliver Lodge, believed that detailed messages had come from his son Raymond, who had been killed at the Front. Many of the bereaved took a very understandable interest in this source of consolation. . . .

## Parapsychology

So from the 1930s a keen interest was taken in the attempts by an American investigator, J.B. Rhine, and others to demonstrate 'extrasensory perception' by experiments in 'parapsychology'. Some still hoped that tests in laboratory conditions would increase confidence in the power to survive death, about which Rhine remained agnostic. The immediate purposes were, however, to examine claims about clairvoyance (the ability to perceive things beyond the range of the senses), precognition (the ability to foresee future events) and psychokinesis (the ability to alter the state of things out of reach). Typical experiments sought to prove an uncanny knowledge of, or control over, numbers, cards and dice. But again interest declined, since few members of the scientific community were willing to grant that the experiments had been conducted according to reliable standards. . . . But some wider objections have also been raised. Why are paranormal powers confined to special occasions? Why is it normally impossible to read a book without opening its covers, or to do physical work without physical effort, or to avoid disasters by accurately predicting dangers without the trouble of scientific research? And if the question about life after death is answered by a reference to 'apparitions', why do not the dead always make themselves known to those who grieve? The conclusion often drawn is that the living brain does indeed have strange powers and memories which deserve recognition and investigation, but that the matter is best left in hands of scientifically minded psychologists. . . .

> *The conclusion often drawn is that the living brain does indeed have strange powers.*

For the purpose of an enquiry into the possibility of life after death, this outcome of modern psychical research seems disappointing. R.W.K. Paterson, who declared himself to be a 'diehard rationalist', has nevertheless decided that the evidence to which he appeals is sufficient to justify belief in a 'plurality of worlds, each created by small groups of interacting selves, with the possibility that an individual self may transfer from one to another according to his current state of consciousness, his character and emotional needs, and the strength of his existing and developing relationships'. But it is difficult to resist the impression that there was something personal, rather than scientific, in his defiant attitude to what he called the 'antecedent improbability' of any survival after death. Moreover, the 'other world' which he envisaged seems suspiciously like a school or university with promotion into a higher class or graduation with honours.

## Near-death experiences

Interest has therefore moved on to reports of experiences more normal than those which had been investigated by psychical research. An American book of 1975 by Raymond Moody, *Life after Life*, drew world-wide attention to the frequency of experiences of 'otherworld journeys' by patients who, usually after being drugged heavily, had been pronounced clinically dead during attempts to resuscitate them in the emergency wards of hospitals (often after cardiac arrests).

Many such patients reported hearing a loud noise which might be music, seeing darkness, floating above the hospital bed, rapidly reviewing their lives with self-criticism, feeling drawn through a tunnel to a brilliant light which at first could be frightening, meeting at least one very friendly 'being of light' and being reunited with 'dead' relatives and friends, before reluctantly accepting a summons back to their bodies. On their return, patients could describe hearing the talk, and seeing the work, of the medical team during the period when they had been thought to be dead. Sometimes they could also report visiting other hospital rooms or seeing objects invisible from their beds.

Also impressive was the frequency with which many people's lives had been transformed by these experiences. People who had been competitive materialists, and often atheists, were now spiritually minded, detached from this-worldly ambitions and cares, far more tolerant, far less likely to think God hostile or dead and far less anxious about the approach of their real deaths. Here seemed to be the evidence which had been long desired, supplied without any motive for fraud and without any dubious attempt to copy tests in scientific laboratories. Paradoxically, it had come as a result of medical technology which had been suspected by some of the spiritually minded; and it had come from people who usually did not claim to be specially 'psychic'. In 1982 a Gallup poll was published which suggested that about eight million Americans had had these experiences.

> *Patients could describe hearing the talk, and seeing the work, of the medical team during the period when they had been thought to be dead.*

Many later publications added to such reports. It was shown that these 'journeys' could be experienced by children, and also by adults who had been born blind. Nor were they made only by modern Christians who identified the 'being of light' as Jesus. Figures of Hindu gods could be seen; parallels could be drawn with *post mortem* journeys into 'the Void' reported in Buddhist texts; stories of 'otherworld journeys' by Christians in the Middle Ages or by shamans in pagan, nonmodern societies were recalled; a British philosopher who remained an atheist, Sir Alfred Ayer, felt the presence of 'guardians' of space and time with the possibility that he might himself 'cure space by operating on time'. Rock-climbers who thought that they were falling to their deaths, and sailors who thought that they were drowning, have also reported a time of a strange calm while they reviewed their lives. And although most of their experiences were joyful, some resuscitated patients reported having had a fearful time, experiencing not usually the fires of traditional pictures of hell but an otherworld of condemnation, humiliation, desolation, chaos and loneliness, sometimes with acute pain. The reports which showed that different kinds of imagery were being used, and that life after death might not be entirely pleasant, seemed only to add to the authenticity of the core discovery, which was (it seemed) that death could be survived by one's spirit. . . .

> *The decision that life after death is a real possibility must involve a belief which falls short of scientific proof.*

However, like the earlier 'findings' of psychical research, these reports can be interpreted without any conclusion that life after death is proved. It can be pointed out that most patients make no claim to have had definite experiences while believed to be dead—and that the stories of those who do make such claims may grow taller in the telling. The emphasis can be on the medical fact that these patients were, after all, not completely dead; if they heard any premature talk about their deaths during their semiconsciousness it was because the power of hearing is one of the last to go when dying. These points have often been accepted and the 'journeys' are now called 'near-death experiences' (or NDEs in the jargon of what has become a large literature), in the same category as the 'out-of-body experiences' familiar to anyone who dreams or daydreams.

The contents of these near-death dreams can be explained within the terms of medical science. Procedures during resuscitations can already be familiar to patients since they are often shown by actors in TV dramas about life in hospitals. During such crises, the brain begins to die because it is starved of oxygen: first uncontrolled hyperactivity and then 'anoxia' account for the semiconscious patient's experiences of noise and darkness. With less input reaching the brain from the senses, and with fewer inhibitions preventing the release of stored memories, what is experienced seems to be specially real although in fact it is all a dream. If the dream is pleasant, the feeling of bliss is the result of the production by a gland of adrenalin and by the brain of opiate-like chemicals known as endorphins, which are known to counteract traumatic stress in other situations; if the dream is a nightmare, that is because the pain caused by the continuing attempts at resuscitation is greater than the tranquillizing effects of the adrenalin and the endorphins. Endorphins do not usually produce hallucinations but the 'light' seen is the growing blank in the centre of the deteriorating mind's picture of reality. The 'beings' seen are memories but are entirely imaginary. The 'floating' with a bird's-eye view is an illusion, as in a dream. Or so it can be explained. What is certain is that the half-alive brain was the instrument which received every impression in these near-death experiences. They, too, might be called by the cautious Chinese 'exceptional body functions'.

It therefore appears that a belief in life after death can be strengthened by the research which has produced evidence that humans have more mental powers than they usually think—and had 'psychical research' been more seriously interested in the history of religion, this belief would have been strengthened by the demonstration that people have more spiritual powers than they usually think. The belief can also be strengthened by the many recent reports that when people are near death they can have reassuring experiences. But the decision that life after death is a real possibility must involve a belief which falls short of scientific proof because it lies outside the scope of science: it belongs not to a laboratory making experiments but to a total view of life. And so the situation remains as it did in 1553, when [French writer] François Rabelais is said to have included among a number of deathbed sayings (which he may have rehearsed in advance) the famous words that he went to seek 'the great Perhaps'.

# 6

# Near Death Experiences Offer Proof of Life After Death

## Elisabeth Kübler-Ross

*Elisabeth Kübler-Ross was a psychiatrist and the author of more than twenty books, including the groundbreaking* On Death and Dying. *Her books have been translated into more than twenty-five languages. She spent most of her life working with the dying and was the recipient of more than twenty honorary doctorates. Kübler-Ross passed away in 2004 at the age of 78.*

Elisabeth Kübler-Ross's work with dying patients offers proof that there is life after death. She has documented many cases of people meeting their dead loved ones, including a Native American woman who saw her dead father at her death and a child who during a near death experience met a dead brother she had not known existed. Her stories demonstrate the existence of life after death.

A long time ago people were much more in touch with the issue of death and believed in Heaven and life after death. It is only in the last hundred years, perhaps, that fewer and fewer people truly know that life exists after our physical body dies. There is no purpose to analyze it at this time and point out why this has occurred. But we are now in a new age and hopefully we have made the transition from an age of science and technology and materialism into a new age of genuine and authentic spirituality. This does not really mean religiosity but spirituality—an awareness that there is something far greater

Elisabeth Kübler-Ross, *The Tunnel and the Light: Essential Insights on Living and Dying with a Letter to a Child with Cancer.* New York: Marlowe & Company, 1999. Copyright © 1999 by The Elisabeth Kübler-Ross Family, LP. All rights reserved. Reproduced by arrangement with The Barbara Hogensen Agency, Inc.

than we are, something that created this universe, created life; that we are an authentic and important and significant part of it, and that we can contribute to its evolution.

All of us, when we were born from the source, from God, have been endowed with this facet of divinity, and that means in a very literal sense that we have a part of that source within us. And that gives us the knowledge of our immortality. Many people are beginning to be aware that the physical body is only the house, or the temple, or—as we call it—the cocoon, which we inherit for a certain number of months or years, until we make the transition called death. Then, at the time of death, we shed this cocoon and we are again as free as butterflies, to use the symbolic language that we use when we talk to dying children and their siblings.

## Mrs. Schwartz

One of my patients helped me to find out how to begin research into finding out what death really is and with it, naturally, the question of life after death. Mrs. Schwartz had been in and out of the intensive care unit fifteen times. Each time she was expected not to survive, and each time she managed to come back. Her husband was a known schizophrenic and each time he had a psychotic episode he tried to kill his youngest son, the youngest of many children. This son was not yet of age and he was the only one still at home. It was the patient's conviction that if she should die prematurely, her husband would lose control, and the life of her youngest son would be in danger. With the help of the Little Aid Society we were able to make arrangements for her to transfer the custody of this child to some relatives. She left the hospital with a great sense of relief and a new freedom, knowing that should she not be able to live long enough, at least her youngest child would be safe.

On one occasion when she became critically ill, she could not get to Chicago where she lived, and was, therefore, admitted to a local hospital in Indiana on an emergency basis.

She remembers being put in a private room. She suddenly sensed that she was only moments away from death, but she could not make up her mind whether she should call the nurse or not. One part of her wanted very much to lean back in the pillows and finally be at peace. But the other part of her needed to make it through one more time, because her youngest son was not yet of age. Before she made the decision to call the nurse and go through this whole rigmarole once more, a nurse apparently walked into her room, took one look at her and dashed out. At this very moment she saw herself slowly and peacefully floating out of her physical body and floating a few feet above her bed. She even had a great sense of humor, relating that her body looked pale and icky. She had a sense of awe and surprise but no fear or anxiety.

She then watched the resuscitation team walk into the room and was able to enumerate in great detail who walked in first, who walked in last. She was totally aware, not only of every word of their conversations, but also of their thought patterns. She even repeated a joke that one of the residents who apparently was very apprehensive started to tell. She had only one great need, namely to tell them to relax, to take it easy, and that she was all right. But the more desperately she tried to convey it, the more frantically they seemed to work on her body until it dawned on her that she was able to perceive them but they were not able to perceive her. Mrs. Schwartz then decided to give up her attempts and, in her own words, "lost consciousness." She was declared dead after forty-five minutes of unsuccessful resuscitation attempts. Three and a half hours later she showed signs of life again, much to the surprise of the hospital staff. She lived another year and a half.

> *At this very moment she saw herself slowly and peacefully floating out of her physical body.*

When Mrs. Schwartz shared this with me and my class in our seminar, it was a brand new experience to me. I had never heard of near-death experiences in spite of the fact that I had been a physician for many years. My students were shocked that I did not call this a hallucination, an illusion or a feeling of depersonalization. They had a desperate need to give it a label, something that they could identify with and then put aside, so as not to have to deal with it.

Mrs. Schwartz's experience, we were sure, could not be a single, unique occurrence. Our hope was to be able to find more cases like this and, perhaps, to go in the direction of collecting data to see if the experience that this patient had had was common, rare, or very unique. The near-death experience has now become known all over the world. Many, many researchers, physicians, psychologists and people who study parapsychological phenomena have collected cases like this, and in the last ten years over twenty-five thousand cases have been collected from all over the world. . . .

## The dead are always with us

Besides an absence of pain and the experience of physical wholeness in a simulated, perfect body, which we may call the ethereal body, people will also be aware that it is impossible to die alone. There are three reasons why no one can die alone. (And this also includes someone who dies of thirst in a desert hundreds of miles from the next human being, or an astronaut missing the target and circling around in the universe until he dies of lack of oxygen.)

> *My students were shocked that I did not call this a hallucination.*

Patients who are slowly preparing themselves for death, as is often the case with children who have cancer, prior to death begin to be aware that they have the ability to leave their physical body and have what we call an "out-of-body" experience. All of us have these out-of-body experiences during certain states of sleep, although very few of us are consciously aware of it. . . .

It is during those out-of-body trips that dying patients become aware of the presence of beings who surround them, who guide them and help them. This is the first reason why you cannot die alone. Young children often refer to them as their playmates. The churches have called them guardian angels. Most researchers would call them guides. It is not important what label we give them. But it is important that we know that from the moment of birth, which begins with the taking of the first breath, until the moment when we make the transition and end of this physical existence, we are in the presence of these guides or guardian angels who will wait for us and help us in the transition from life to life after death.

The second reason why we cannot die alone is that we will

always be met by those who preceded us in death and whom we have loved—a child we have lost, perhaps decades earlier, a grandmother, a father, a mother or other people who have been significant in our lives. . . .

The third reason why we cannot die alone is that when we shed our physical bodies even temporarily prior to death, we are in an existence where there is no time and no space. And in this existence we can be anywhere we choose to be at the speed of our thought. A young man who dies in Viet Nam and thinks of his mother in Chicago will be in Chicago with the speed of his thought. . . .

## Seeing dead relatives

It is interesting to me as a psychiatrist that thousands of people all around the globe should share the same hallucinations prior to death; namely, the awareness of some relatives or friends who preceded them in death. There must be some explanation for this if it's not real. And so I proceeded to try to find out means and ways to study this, to verify this. Or perhaps to verify that it is simply a projection of wishful thinking. The best way perhaps to study it is for us to sit with dying children after family accidents. We usually did this after the 4th of July, weekends, Memorial Days, Labor Days, when families go out together in family cars and all too often have head-on collisions, killing several members of the family and sending many of the injured survivors into different hospitals.

> *We will always be met by those who preceded us in death and whom we have loved.*

I have made it a task to sit with the critically injured children since they are my specialty. As is usually the case, they have not been told which of their family members were killed in the same accident. I was always impressed that they were invariably aware of who had preceded them in death anyway!

I sit with them, watch them silently, perhaps hold their hand, watch their restlessness and then, often shortly prior to death, a peaceful serenity comes over them. That is always an ominous sign. And that is the moment when I communicate with them. And I don't give them any ideas. I simply ask them if they are willing and able to share with me what they experience. They share in very similar words.

As one child said to me, "Everything is all right now. Mommy and Peter are already waiting for me."

I was aware in this particular case that the mother had been killed immediately at the scene of the accident. But I also knew that Peter had gone to a burn unit in a different hospital and that he, as far as I knew, was still alive. I didn't give it a second thought, but as I walked out of the intensive care unit by the nursing station, I had a telephone call from the hospital where Peter was. The nurse at the other end of the line said, "Dr. Ross, we just wanted to tell you that Peter died ten minutes ago."

The only mistake I made was to say, "Yes, I know." The nurse might have thought that I was a little coo-coo.

> *One child said to me, 'Everything is all right now. Mommy and Peter are already waiting for me.'*

In thirteen years of studying children near death I have never had one child who has made a single mistake when it comes to identifying—in this way—family members who have preceded them in death. I would like to see statistics on that.

There's another experience that perhaps moved me even more, and that was a case of an American Indian woman. She told me that her sister had been killed hundreds of miles away from the reservation by a hit-and-run driver. Another car stopped and the driver tried to help her. The dying woman told the stranger that he should make very, very sure to tell her mother that she was all right because she was with her father. She died after having shared that. The patient's father had died one hour before this accident on the reservation, seven hundred miles away from the accident scene and certainly unbeknownst to his traveling daughter. . . .

## Returning from the afterlife

There is also the case of a man who lost his entire family in a car accident in which they were all burned to death. Because of this terrible loss he turned from a money-earning, decent middle class husband and father to a total bum, who was drunk every day from morning till night and was using every conceivable drug in order to commit suicide, and yet never was able to succeed.

> *Our physical body is only a shell that encloses our immortal self.*

His last recollection was how he was lying on the edge of a forest in a dirt road, drunk and "stoned" as he called it, wanting to be reunited with his family, not wanting to live, not having the energy to even move out of the road, when he saw a big truck coming down the street and literally run over him. At this moment he watched himself in the street, critically injured, while he observed the whole scene of the accident a few feet from above, as he called it.

It was at this moment that his family appeared in front of him in a glow of light with an incredible sense of love and happy smiles on their faces, simply making him aware of their presence, not communicating in any verbal way, but in a form of a thought transference, sharing with him the joy and the happiness of their present existence.

This man was not able to tell us how long this reunion was going on, but he was so awed by their health, their beauty and radiance, by their total acceptance of his present-life situation, by their unconditional love, that he made a vow not to touch them, not to join them, but to re-enter his physical body and to promise that he would share with the world what he had experienced—in a form of a redemption for his two years of trying to throw his physical life away.

It was after this vow that he watched how the truck driver carried his injured body into the car, how an ambulance was speeding up to the scene of the accident, how he was taken to the hospital emergency room and strapped down on a stretcher. And it was in the emergency room that he finally re-entered his physical body, tore off the straps that were tied around him, and walked out of the emergency room without ever having any delirium tremens or any after effects from his heavy abuse of drugs and alcohol. He felt healed and whole and made a commitment that he would not die until he had the opportunity of sharing the existence of life after death with as many people as were willing to hear him.

We do not know what has happened to this man since then. But I will never forget the glow in his eyes, the joy and the deep gratitude he experienced when he was allowed to stand up on a stage in one of my workshops and share with a group of hundreds of hospice workers the total knowledge and awareness that our physical body is only a shell that encloses our immortal self.

# 7

# Near Death Experiences Do Not Prove Life After Death

## Susan Blackmore

*Susan Blackmore is a freelance writer, a broadcaster, and a visiting lecturer at the University of the West of England in Bristol. She has a degree in psychology and physiology from Oxford University and a doctorate in parapsychology from the University of Surrey. She has written several books in-cluding* Dying to Live *and* In Search of the Light.

Near death experiences (NDEs) do not provide evidence for life after death. Although they seem completely real and can transform people's lives, they are the result of the natural processes of a dying brain. For example, the common vision of a tunnel of light is created by the brain when it lacks oxygen. People's experiences of see-ing excerpts of their lives flashing before them are also a normal effect caused by a dying brain. Once the brain has died, these visions cease and the person experienc-ing them dies as well.

Resuscitation from ever more serious heart failure has pro-vided accounts of extraordinary experiences (although this is not the only cause of NDEs [near death experiences]). These remained largely ignored until about 15 years ago, when Ray-mond Moody (1975), an American physician, published his best-selling *Life After Life*. He had talked with many people who had "come back from death," and he put together an account of a typical NDE. In this idealized experience a person hears

Susan Blackmore, "Near-Death Experiences: In or Out of the Body?" *Skeptical In-quirer*, vol. 16, Fall 1991, pp. 34–45. Copyright © 1991 by the Committee for the Scientific Investigation of Claims of the Paranormal. Reproduced by permission.

himself pronounced dead. Then comes a loud buzzing or ringing noise and a long, dark tunnel. He can see his own body from a distance and watch what is happening. Soon he meets others and a "being of light" who shows him a playback of events from his life and helps him to evaluate it. At some point he gets to a barrier and knows that he has to go back. Even though he feels joy, love, and peace there, he returns to his body and life. Later he tries to tell others; but they don't understand, and he soon gives up. Nevertheless the experience deeply affects him, especially his views about life and death.

> *About 1 in 7 adult Americans had been close to death.*

Many scientists reacted with disbelief. They assumed Moody was at least exaggerating, but he claimed that no one had noticed the experiences before because the patients were too frightened to talk about them. The matter was soon settled by further research. One cardiologist had talked to more than 2,000 people over a period of nearly 20 years and claimed that more than half reported Moody-type experiences. In 1982, a Gallup poll found that about 1 in 7 adult Americans had been close to death and about 1 in 20 had had an NDE. It appeared that Moody, at least in outline, was right. . . .

## Typical NDEs

Within a few years some of the basic questions were being answered. Kenneth Ring (1980), at the University of Connecticut, surveyed 102 people who had come close to death and found almost 50 percent had had what he called a "core experience." He broke this into five stages: peace, body separation, entering the darkness (which is like the tunnel), seeing the light, and entering the light. He found that the later stages were reached by fewer people, which seems to imply that there is an ordered set of experiences waiting to unfold.

One interesting question is whether NDEs are culture specific. What little research there is suggests that in other cultures NDEs have basically the same structure, although religious background seems to influence the way it is interpreted. A few

NDEs have even been recorded in children. It is interesting to note that nowadays children are more likely to see living friends than those who have died, presumably because their playmates only rarely die of diseases like scarlet fever or smallpox.

Perhaps more important is whether you have to be nearly dead to have an NDE. The answer is clearly no. Many very similar experiences are recorded of people who have taken certain drugs, were extremely tired, or, occasionally, were just carrying on their ordinary activities.

I must emphasize that these experiences seem completely real—even more real (whatever that may mean) than everyday life. The tunnel experience is not like just imagining going along a tunnel. The view from out of the body seems completely realistic, not like a dream, but as though you really are up there and looking down. Few people experience such profound emotions and insight again during their lifetimes. They do not say, "I've been hallucinating," "I imagined I went to heaven," or "Can I tell you about my lovely dream?" They are more likely to say, "I have been out of my body" or "I saw Grandma in heaven."

> *The experience of seeing excerpts from your life flash before you is not really as mysterious as it first seems.*

Since not everyone who comes close to death has an NDE, it is interesting to ask what sort of people are more likely to have them. Certainly you don't need to be mentally unstable. NDEers do not differ from others in terms of their psychological health or background. Moreover, the NDE does seem to produce profound and positive personality changes. After this extraordinary experience people claim that they are no longer so motivated by greed and material achievement but are more concerned about other people and their needs. Any theory of the NDE needs to account for this effect. . . .

## "Just hallucinations"

Perhaps we should give up and conclude that all the experiences are "just imagination" or "nothing but hallucinations." However, this is the weakest theory of all. The experiences must, in some sense, be hallucinations, but this is not, on its own, any explanation. We have to ask why are they these kinds of hallucinations? Why tunnels?

Some say the tunnel is a symbolic representation of the gateway to another world. But then why always a tunnel and not, say, a gate, doorway, or even the great River Styx? Why the light at the end of the tunnel? And why always above the body, not below it? I have no objection to the theory that the experiences are hallucinations. I only object to the idea that you can explain them by saying, "They are just hallucinations." This explains nothing. A viable theory would answer these questions without dismissing the experiences. That, even if only in tentative form, is what I shall try to provide.

## The physiology of the tunnel

Tunnels do not only occur near death. They are also experienced in epilepsy and migraine, when falling asleep, meditating, or just relaxing, with pressure on both eyeballs, and with certain drugs, such as LSD, psilocybin, and mescaline. I have experienced them many times myself. It is as though the whole world becomes a rushing, roaring tunnel and you are flying along it toward a bright light at the end. No doubt many readers have also been there, for surveys show that about a third of people have—like this terrified man of 28 who had just had the anesthetic for a circumcision.

> I seemed to be hauled at "lightning speed" in a direct line tunnel into outer space; (not a floating sensation . . .) but like a rocket at a terrific speed. I appeared to have left my body.

In the 1930s, Heinrich Kluver, at the University of Chicago, noted four form constants in hallucinations: the tunnel, the spiral, the lattice or grating, and the cobweb. Their origin probably lies in the structure of the visual cortex, the part of the brain that processes visual information. Imagine that the outside world is mapped onto the back of the eye (on the retina), and then again in the cortex. The mathematics of this mapping (at least to a reasonable approximation) is well known.

Jack Cowan, a neurobiologist at the University of Chicago, has used this mapping to account for the tunnel. Brain activity is normally kept stable by some cells inhibiting others. Disinhibition (the reduction of this inhibitory activity) produces too much activity in the brain. This can occur near death (because of lack of oxygen) or with drugs like LSD, which interfere with inhibition. Cowan uses an analogy with fluid mechanics to argue that disinhibition will induce stripes of activity that move across the cortex. Using the mapping it can easily be shown that stripes in the cortex would appear like concentric rings or spirals in the visual world. In other words, if you have stripes in the cortex you will seem to see a tunnel-like pattern of spirals or rings. . . .

## The life review

The experience of seeing excerpts from your life flash before you is not really as mysterious as it first seems. It has long been known that stimulation of cells in the temporal lobe of the brain can produce instant experiences that seem like the reliving of memories. Also, temporal-lobe epilepsy can produce similar experiences, and such seizures can involve other limbic structures in the brain, such as the amygdala and hippocampus, which are also associated with memory.

Imagine that the noise in the dying brain stimulates cells like this. The memories will be aroused and, according to my hypothesis, if they are the most stable model the system has at that time they will seem real. For the dying person they may well be more stable than the confused and noisy sensory model.

The link between temporal-lobe epilepsy and the NDE has

*In this state the outside world is no longer real, and inner worlds are.*

formed the basis of a thorough neurobiological model of the NDE. [Scholars J.C. Saavedra-Aguilar and J.S. Gomez-Jeria] suggest that the brain stress consequent on the near-death episode leads to the release of neuropeptides and neurotransmitters (in particular the endogenous endorphins). These then stimulate the limbic system and other connected areas. In addition, the effect of the endorphins could account for the blissful and other positive emotional states so often associated with the NDE. . . .

Of course there is more to the life review than just memories. The person feels as though she or he is judging these life events, being shown their significance and meaning. But this too, I suggest, is not so very strange. When the normal world of the senses is gone and memories seem real, our perspective on our life changes. We can no longer be so attached to our plans, hopes, ambitions, and fears, which fade away and become unimportant, while the past comes to life again. We can only accept it as it is, and there is no one to judge it but ourselves. This is, I think, why so many NDEers say they faced their past life with acceptance and equanimity.

> *** This profound experience leaves its mark. **

Now we come to what might seem the most extraordinary parts of the NDE: the worlds beyond the tunnel and OBE [out-of-body experience]. But I think you can now see that they are not so extraordinary at all. In this state the outside world is no longer real, and inner worlds are. Whatever we can imagine clearly enough will seem real. And what will we imagine when we know we are dying? I am sure for many people it is the world they expect or hope to see. Their minds may turn to people they have known who have died before them or to the world they hope to enter next. Like the other images we have been considering, these will seem perfectly real.

Finally, there are those aspects of the NDE that are ineffable—they cannot be put into words. I suspect that this is because some people take yet another step, a step into nonbeing. I shall try to explain this by asking another question. What is consciousness? If you say it is a thing, another body, a substance, you will only get into the kinds of difficulty we got into with OBEs. I prefer to say that consciousness is just what it is like being a mental model. In other words, all the mental models in any person's mind are all conscious, but only one is a model of "me." This is the one that I think of as myself and to which I relate everything else. It gives a core to my life. It allows me to think that I am a person, something that lives on all the time. It allows me to ignore the fact that "I" change from moment to moment and even disappear every night in sleep.

Now when the brain comes close to death, this model of self may simply fall apart. Now there is no self. It is a strange and dramatic experience. For there is no longer an experiencer—yet there is experience.

This state is obviously hard to describe, for the "you" who is trying to describe it cannot imagine not being. Yet this profound experience leaves its mark. The self never seems quite the same again.

## The aftereffects

I think we can now see why an essentially physiological event can change people's lives so profoundly. The experience has jolted their usual (and erroneous) view of the relationship between themselves and the world. We all too easily assume that we are some kind of persistent entity inhabiting a perishable body. But, as the Buddha taught we have to see through that illusion. The world is only a construction of an information-processing system, and the self is too. I believe that the NDE gives people a glimpse into the nature of their own minds that is hard to get any other way. Drugs can produce it temporarily, mystical experiences can do it for rare people, and long years of practice in meditation or mindfulness can do it. But the NDE can out of the blue strike anyone and show them what they never knew before, that their body is only that—a lump of flesh—that they are not so very important after all. And that is a very freeing and enlightening experience.

## And afterwards?

If my analysis of the NDE is correct, we can extrapolate to the next stage. Lack of oxygen first produces increased activity through disinhibition, but eventually it all stops. Since it is this activity that produces the mental models that give rise to consciousness, then all this will cease. There will be no more experience, no more self, and so that, as far as my constructed self is concerned, is the end.

# 8

# Mediums Can Speak with the Dead

## Gary E. Schwartz

*Gary E. Schwartz is a professor of psychology, medicine, neurology, psychiatry, and surgery at the University of Arizona, and director of its Human Energy Systems Laboratory. After receiving his doctorate from Harvard University, he served as a professor of psychology and psychiatry at Yale University, director of the Yale Psychophysiology Center, and codirector of the Yale Behavioral Medicine Clinic. He has published more than four hundred scientific papers and edited eleven academic books. He is also the author of* The Afterlife Experiments: Breakthrough Scientific Evidence of Life After Death.

In an experiment to investigate the afterlife, a medium conducted individual readings of various people, called sitters, over the phone. These readings consisted of images, names, and places that formed in the medium's mind about the sitter. The medium did not know the sitters she read for, and the phone was muted so that she could not make statements based on the reactions of her sitters. All of the information came to the medium through dead people whom the sitter had been close to. The medium's interaction with the dead proves that there is life after death.

W hen a scientific experiment is being considered, the researchers and the scientists involved in the project make decisions about what's required, which procedures will be most appropriate, and how to go about accomplishing what's needed.

Gary E. Schwartz, with William L. Simon, *The Afterlife Experiments: Breakthrough Scientific Evidence of Life After Death.* New York: Pocket Books, 2002. Copyright © 2002 by Gary E. Schwartz, PhD, William L. Simon, and Linda G. Russek, PhD. All rights reserved. Reproduced by permission of Pocket Books, an imprint of Simon & Schuster, Inc.

That's the usual way. [This] experiment wouldn't include much that was "usual" about it.

Laurie Campbell mentioned while visiting us one day in December 2000 that she had been using a novel procedure at home in her telephone readings with clients. She had begun to notice that she was receiving information even before a reading got under way—specific information such as names, relationships, causes of death, personal descriptions. A lightbulb went on; she had started doing a "pre-reading" in which she would meditate for fifteen minutes or half an hour before beginning a reading, and write down whatever information came to her during that period.

> *Of the three readings, the most striking was the one in which we had arranged for the sitter to be another medium, George Dalzell.*

When the call came in from the sitter [the person Laurie was reading], Laurie would explain how she conducts a reading and then would go over what she had received in the meditation period. Only after that would she begin the usual reading.

At the time we learned this, Laurie had already collected data on more than a hundred sitters, and said that her accuracy rates on the pre-reading data were ranging between 50 percent and 95 percent.

I came to term this design the Campbell Procedure to acknowledge that Laurie had come up with the idea herself. It seemed to be an extension of the Russek Procedure [a psychic reading over the phone], where the first ten minutes of the readings are conducted in complete silence.

Needless to say, Linda [another researcher] and I were eager to test Laurie's idea in the laboratory, and we conceived a controlled, blinded experiment to investigate her claims. The idea was to combine the Russek Procedure and the Campbell Procedure in the same experiment.

The data gathering took place soon after, in Tucson [Arizona], on Sunday, December 20. Three sitters were used, from various locations, and they each agreed to remain at home, ready to participate. Extreme care was taken from the first to insure that no one but the experimenters knew the sitters' identity. Laurie stayed at our house, where we were able to observe her, and she had no cell phone or other communication device we could detect.

The plan was fairly straightforward. Half an hour before a scheduled reading, Laurie would meditate, in seclusion and in silence, and would then write down the impressions she received during this meditation period. With the sitters each at some distant location, all possible cues—visible, auditory, even olfactory—were eliminated. That appeared to totally rule out any accusations of cold reading, subtle cueing, or medium fraud as possible explanations of the findings.

After about a half hour of pre-reading, we established telephone contact with the scheduled sitter. A Sony digital video-tape recorder was used to record the initial reception of the sitter and the conduct of the Russek Procedure.

The sitter was reminded that the phone would momentarily be placed on mute (so that the sitter would not be able to hear Laurie speaking), and that for the duration of the ten-minute silent-sitter period the person was to hold the phone to his or her ear. Each time before passing the muted phone to Laurie, we checked to make sure that the mute button was working to cut off the sound, and that neither Laurie nor the sitter could hear any voices.

With mute activated, the handset was passed to Laurie, who chose to hold the phone turned away from her ear to minimize any noises or static on the phone line.

> *George had 'invited' four deceased people to participate.*

The Sony video camera recorded the ten-minute Russek Procedure while Laurie described out loud the impressions she was receiving. At no time did the experimenters refer to the sitter by name, and of course Laurie had not yet heard the sitter's voice.

On completion of the sitter-silent period, the phone was taken off mute, and Laurie then introduced herself and explained how she conducted a normal medium/sitter dialogue reading. She then read, item by item, the notes she had made from the pre-reading contemplation, and asked the sitter to confirm, question, or contradict the information.

What we most wanted to know was whether Laurie would be able to generate discrete and specific accurate information during the pre-reading period.

## The George Dalzell reading

Of the three readings, the most striking was the one in which we had arranged for the sitter to be another medium, George Dalzell. He was a uniquely appropriate choice for several reasons. A professionally trained and licensed clinical social worker, he comes from a highly educated academic family. He himself was educated at Northwestern University in Chicago, and his father, grandfather, and great-grandfather were educated at Yale University. And he has been active as a medium for the past few years—but in secret, for fear of endangering his professional standing in the social work community.

At the time of testing, Laurie and George had never met face to face, nor had they communicated by phone, fax, mail, or e-mail. Laurie was aware of George and knew that he worked as medium, but she was not informed that he would be one of the sitters selected to participate in this experiment.

George had "invited" four deceased people to participate. A plethora of documented information would be available to us; we could easily verify the data that Laurie might receive.

The session with George took over an hour. After Laurie's meditation period, she wrote down that the sitter (who had yet to be telephoned) was concerned with "truth that is held within the soul's journey—journey of the soul's path—truth from someone with an M name" and that the sitter was preparing to "stand up and be counted." She also wrote the names George, Michael, Alice, Bob, and Jerry, and mentions of "a small dog" and "candles burning."

We would soon learn that *every one* of the names of the deceased people invited by George was absolutely correct. In particular, she had received George's own name and the name of his best friend, Michael, who had recently passed. George had lit a candle just before the beginning of the experiment—something that, he said, he very rarely does. About the "stand up and be counted," though this might be a stretch, there is a sense in which we knew he was at the time preparing to do this: he had written a book, *Messages*, about his experiences as a medium and was looking forward to having it published.

During the Russek Procedure silent period—with Laurie

holding the phone but still not having heard the voice of the person on the other end—she produced a large amount of data.

By now we had experienced over and over mediums producing large amount of correct information—nothing new about that. The crucial distinction here lay in the sitter's not being in the same room—the sitter and medium in fact being in two different parts of the country with no contact at all or, at most, connected only over a muted telephone. This would seem to answer the doubts of even the most suspicious skeptic.

The amount of totally correct information Laurie reported was mind-boggling. All these statements were correct: That the reading was for a person named George and that the primary deceased person was Michael. That there was an East Coast and a California connection (George comes from the East Coast, and he currently lives in California). That his father is deceased. That both he and his father have had connections with science and with books.

And more: That Alice was the name of an aunt. That there was a dog, and it had an "S" name. And that there was someone with a strange name that sounded like "Talya," "Tiya," or "Tilya."

Still, as usual, the reading was by no means perfect. Some of the statements were general and could apply to many people—for example, that the sitter was loving and caring. And she made outright mistakes, such as that George's mother was deceased, when in fact she was living and in good health.

> ❝ The precision of the details, and their accuracy, was simply awesome. ❞

When the reading proper began—both people on the phone and able to speak to each other—Laurie first reviewed the pre-reading information she had received, and then started the reading by mentioning that someone named Jerry had passed recently, and that Michael was a "partner" to George, and George's "muse." She described Michael's personality accurately—not only as loving and caring, but obsessively neat and "pristine"—all correct, and George particularly agreed that "pristine" was an accurate description. She saw him in a white kitchen that was cozy and done with stone, also correct.

Laurie then moved to Jerry. She saw him from the Brook-lyn area. Once again, here was a fact that the sitter, George, did not know about his friend but was able to confirm after the reading. Laurie saw him as sitting on bar stools, drinking and smoking, and often intoxicated, but that he had stopped drink-ing before he died. Every one of these statements was right on the money.

> **//** *Any skeptic watching the videotape of this experiment would have great difficulty explaining how Laurie came to mention the presence of three scientists.* **//**

Even more remarkable, I thought, were statements by Lau-rie that Michael showed her where he had lived somewhere in Europe; he showed her a big city and then was traveling through the countryside to his home. Along the road to his house Laurie was shown a river, an old stone monastery on the edge of the river, and "centuries-old stonework." She reported his parents as having heavy accent.

George had visited Michael at his parents' home in Ger-many and knew Michael's parents did indeed speak English with a heavy accent. He could also confirm the parts about the big city, the countryside, the road to his home alongside a river, and their living in a village. However, he did not recall any-thing about an old stone monastery along the river.

Laurie then described the older Aunt A, her great sense of humor (true) but related that A was experiencing "compassion and sorrow" for her granddaughter (true). Laurie correctly gave the exact name of the granddaughter, who she said was having difficulty, was "uncontrolled," and was currently receiving "healing."

George was unaware of any such situation.

Moving back to George himself, Laurie said she was being shown by Michael that George's life was about to become "noisy" and be "turned upside down." Indeed, with the publi-cation of George's book, his secret life as a medium would be-come a matter of public record, and he might have to face pro-fessional complications in his role as a psychiatric social worker in good standing with the Los Angeles County Department of

Mental Health, or with his other job as psychiatric admissions coordinator at a hospital in Glendale, California.

Laurie reported Michael showing her George and "white-coat" clinicians in a hospital. It turned out that George had performed psychological evaluations in the emergency room of a Los Angeles hospital just before the reading.

She described a small dog—description of personality and colors reported by George to be accurate—and saw the dog being near a favorite tree and water. George later informed us that he and his dog had spent many hours at a special tree near the water, where his former dog was buried.

There have been times in this work when it has been difficult to retain a scientific detachment. This was certainly one of them. The precision of the details, and their accuracy, was simply awesome. . . .

Laurie Campbell, the housewife who had at first been worried about trying to do readings in the company of esteemed mediums with national reputations, had accomplished a feat of mediumship that may well be remembered in the history of the field.

## Scoring the readings

The formal scoring of these readings showed that two of the three were in every way up to the standards of what we had come to expect.

The third, with George Dalzell, not only met that standard but went far beyond it. Laurie had provided over a hundred specific details, with an accuracy that ranged between 90 percent and 100 percent per deceased person. . . .

Of the thirty-one names or variations Laurie reported, only three had no connection at all with George, while thirteen were absolutely accurate. . . .

One curiosity is noted for the sake of completeness and integrity. In the actual reading phase, Laurie brought up the names of three deceased well-known scientists. George later advised us that he had also invited "spirit scientists" to help facilitate the experiment, without specifying any particular people. She gave the names of Albert Einstein, Carl Jung, and David Bohm (an internationally renowned physicist who had once taught at Princeton, but a name Laurie could hardly have been expected to know).

Any skeptic watching the videotape of this experiment

would have great difficulty explaining how Laurie came to mention the presence of three scientists—something she had never done in the context of any previous research reading since we had begun our work with her three years earlier.

## Summing up

The new method we had termed the Campbell Procedure blocks any possibility of input from the sitter of the kind relied on by cold readers—anything that might suggest whether a particular statement is close to the truth or out in left field. Not even an inadvertent noise like a shuffling of body position or an unconscious sucking in of breath would become a clue.

Also, the procedures used in this experiment completely answered the issues that psychic magician Ross Horowitz had raised. Even if the medium or an investigator working for her had found out in advance who the sitters would be, Laurie could not know which person we had dialed.

George later wrote: "If you score the reading overall on the basis of naming the intended spirit collaborators, Laurie scored with 100 percent accuracy. . . . It was one of the great thrills of my life to have a medium bring through my Aunt Alice, who was the dearest love in my life, like a second mother to me—and with such strength and accuracy in the reading."

Linda and I were elated. In our most persuasive experiment to date, in terms of safeguards against deceit or trickery, this procedure seemed to answer almost every challenge a skeptic could throw at us.

# 9

# There Is No Evidence That Mediums Can Speak with the Dead

Ray Hyman

*Ray Hyman is a professor emeritus of psychology at the University of Oregon. His lifelong research interests include examination of alleged psychic readings and the psychology of deception and self-deception. His book* The Elusive Quarry *is a collection of his examinations of parapsychological experiments.*

Gary E. Schwartz attempted to provide scientific evidence for life after death by proving that people with psychic abilities, called mediums, are able to speak with the dead. His research, however, is flawed in numerous ways. Rather than following strict scientific methodology, his study contains biased information and opinion. For example, it was up to the sitters, or people being read by the medium, to decide whether or not the medium was communicating with the dead. Sitters who already believed in life after death were predisposed to believe that the medium was getting messages about them from the dead. This flaw and others invalidate Schwartz's research claims.

S ince 1997, [Gary E.] Schwartz has reported a number of studies in which he and his coworkers have observed some talented mediums such as John Edward and George Anderson give readings to sitters in his laboratory. This work has attracted considerable attention because of Schwartz's credentials and

Ray Hyman, "How Not to Test Mediums: Critiquing the Afterlife Experiments," *Skeptical Inquirer*, vol. 27, January/February 2003, pp. 20–30. Copyright © 2003 by the Committee for the Scientific Investigation of Claims of the Paranormal. Reproduced by permission.

position. Even more eye-opening is Schwartz's apparent endorsement of the mediums' claims that they are actually communicating with the dead. . . .

Schwartz's new book *The Afterlife Experiments* presents evidence from a series of five reports in which Schwartz and his associates observed mediums give readings to sitters "in stringently monitored experiments." Schwartz does admit that his experiments were not ideal. For example, only the very last in his sequence of studies used a truly double-blind format.[1] Yet he insists that the mediums, although often wrong, consistently came up with specific facts and names about the sitters' departed friends and relatives that the skeptics have been unable to explain away as fraud, cold reading,[2] or lucky guesses. He provides several examples of such instances throughout the book. These examples demonstrate, he believes, that the readings given by his mediums are clearly different from those given by cold readers and less gifted psychics. "If cold readings are easy to spot by anyone familiar with the techniques, the kinds of readings we have been getting," he asserts, "in our laboratory are quite different in character.". . .

## Cold readings

A number of factors . . . can make an ambiguous reading seem highly specific, unique, and uncannily accurate. And once the observer or client has been struck with the apparent accuracy of the reading, it becomes virtually impossible to dislodge the belief in the uniqueness and specificity of the reading. Research from many areas demonstrates this finding. . . .

Again and again, Schwartz argues that the readings given by his star mediums differ greatly from cold readings. He provides samples of readings throughout the book. Although these samples were obviously selected because, in his opinion, they represent mediumship at its best, every one of them strikes me as no different in kind from those of any run-of-the-mill psychic reader and as completely consistent with cold readings. . . .

I am sure that Professor Schwartz will strongly disagree with my observation that the readings he presents as strong evidence for his case very much resemble the sorts of readings we

---

1. a format where neither the sitter nor the medium has information available that can influence results    2. gathering information by asking common questions and using the answers to make educated guesses that seem like a psychic reading

would expect from psychic readers in general and cold readers in particular. This disagreement between us, however, relies on subjective assessment. That is why we have widely accepted scientific methods to settle the issue. That is why it is important, especially for the sort of revolutionary claims that Schwartz wants to make, that it be backed up by competent scientific evidence. Throughout his 2002 book *The Afterlife Experiments*, Schwartz implies that he has already provided such evidence.

This, as I will explain, is badly mistaken. The research he presents is flawed. Probably no other extended program in psychical research deviates so much from accepted norms of scientific methodology as this one does.

## Flawed control groups

Although never going so far as to claim his research methodology is ideal, [Schwartz] apparently believes it is adequate to justify his conclusions that his mediums are communicating with the dead. He writes, "Skeptics who claim that this is some kind of fraud the mediums are working on us have nonetheless been unable to point out any error in our experimental technique to account for the results." Later he asserts, "The data appear to be real. If there is a fundamental flaw in the totality of the research presented in these pages, the flaw has managed to escape the many experienced scientists who have carefully examined the work to date.". . .

> **"** *Schwartz does admit that his experiments were not ideal.* **"**

If [Schwartz] wants to claim scientific acceptance for his evidence then he has to gather the data under conditions that eliminate or adequately correct for [any] bias. Even worse is his rejoinder to the claim that he used an inappropriate control group. "The purpose of the original . . . experiments was *not* to include an ideal control group, but rather to address, and possibly rule out (or in) one possible explanation for the data—i.e., simple guessing."

This last statement is both confusing and wrong. I suspect that Schwartz means by "an ideal control group" one made up of individuals who are the same age and have the same sort of experience as his mediums. Since his actual control group consisted of undergraduate students who had no prior experience as mediums, the group was obviously not ideal in this sense. . . . This control group in no way provides a proper comparison or baseline for the "accuracy ratings" of the mediums by the sitters. This is for the simple reason that the control group was given a task that differed in very important ways from that of the mediums. There is no way that the results from this control group could provide a comparison or baseline for simple guessing.

> *A number of factors . . . can make an ambiguous reading seem highly specific, unique, and uncannily accurate.*

The mediums are free to make statements about possible contacts, names, relations, causes of death, and other matters. In the earlier experiments they were given "yes" and "no" replies from the sitters and in later experiments they typically began a segment without feedback and then went through an additional segment with feedback. The sitters were free to find matches within the output of the medium to fit their particular circumstances. Later the sitter was given a transcript of the entire reading and rated each statement for how accurately it applied to her situation. The statements that got the highest rating were counted as hits. The proportion of such hits varied from approximately 73 to 90 percent in the earlier experiments and somewhat lower in the later ones.

In contrast, the control subjects were given a series of questions based on a reading given to their first sitter. Statements from the readings were converted into questions that could be answered in such a way that the answer could be scored correct or incorrect. For example, if the medium had correctly guessed the cause of the sitter's mother's death, a question given to the controls might be, "What was the cause of her mother's death?" Schwartz and his colleagues report that the average percentage of correct answers by the controls was 36 percent. Because the "accuracy" of the mediums was much higher, the researchers conclude that the mediums had access to true information that cannot be explained away as guessing. . . .

This is an inappropriate comparison. Although Schwartz claims that, if anything, the controls had an advantage over the mediums, the use of the results for the control groups as a baseline for the mediums is completely meaningless. [Researchers] Wiseman and O'Keeffe provide several reasons why. In addition to the reasons they give, a more fundamental one is that the score for the controls does not involve subjective ratings by the sitters *while the accuracy scores for the mediums depend entirely upon the judgment of these sitters*. We have no idea how well the mediums could do if given the same task as the controls. I strongly suspect they could not perform any better. . . .

## White crows

[Schwartz's] book begins with a quotation from [psychologist] William James. "In order to disprove the law that all crows are black, it is enough to find one white crow." James was interested in the possibility of psychic phenomena. He believed that it was sufficient to find one truly indisputable example of a psychic occurrence to demonstrate that violations of natural law were possible. Schwartz claims he has uncovered several white crows. The performance of his mediums, especially Laurie Campbell and John Edward, earn them the accolade in his judgment, of "white crow" mediums. He has also found at least one "white crow" sitter in one of his participants, GD. . . .

## A double-blind experiment

[Schwartz] and his colleagues finally conducted a double-blind experiment using Campbell as the medium and six sitters, one of whom was GD. During the readings, Campbell and the sitters had no contact and the two experimenters who were with Campbell were blind to the order in which the sitters were run. Later each sitter was sent two transcripts to judge. One was of the actual reading for that sitter and the other was of a reading given to another subject. The sitters were given no clues as to which was their actual reading. "The question was, even under blind conditions, could the sitters determine which of the readings was theirs?" . . .

Schwartz believes this double-blind experiment has put to rest all the skeptical arguments against his evidence. One of Schwartz's mantras in relation to his afterlife experiments is *let the data speak*. When I read the full report of this "ultimate 'white crow' design," the data did speak loud and clear. However, the story the data told is just the opposite from the one that Professor Schwartz apparently hears.

> **The research [Schwartz] presents is flawed.**

The plan of the study was admirably simple. Campbell gave readings to the six sitters in an order that neither she nor the experimenter who was with her knew. In this way neither the medium nor the person in her presence was aware of who the sitter was at the time of the reading. At the time of the reading, the sitter was physically separated from the medium. The medium gave her readings in Tucson, Arizona, while the sitters were in their homes in different parts of the country. Subsequently, each sitter was mailed two transcripts. One of the transcripts was the actual reading for that sitter and the other was from the reading of another sitter. Each sitter rated the two transcripts, not knowing which was the one actually intended for her or him, according to instructions provided by the researchers. The sitter first circled every item in the transcripts which they judged to be a "dazzle shot." "For you, a dazzle shot is some piece of information—whatever it is *to you*, that you experience as 'right on' or 'wow' or 'that's my family.'" Next, the sitter was instructed to go through the transcripts again and score each item as a hit, a miss, or unsure.

Finally, the sitter designated which of the two transcripts was the one that actually was intended for him or her.

The hypothesis was that if Campbell could truly access information from the sitter's departed acquaintances, this would show up on all three measures. In other words, the sitters would successfully pick their own reading from the two transcripts: they would record significantly more dazzle shots in their own transcripts as compared with the control transcripts; and they would find many more hits and fewer misses in the actual as opposed to the control transcript. *Each one of these three predictions failed.* Four of the sitters did correctly pick their own transcript, but this is consistent with the chance expectation of three successes. On the two more sensitive measures, there were no significant differences in number of dazzle shots or hits and misses.

The authors admit that for the overall data, "there was no apparent evidence of a reliable anomalous information retrieval effect." So how can they use these results to proclaim a "breathtaking" vindication of their previous findings? This is because, when they looked at the results separately for each sitter, they discovered that in the case of GD, who had been the star sitter in a previous experiment with Campbell, he not only successfully identified his own transcript but also found nine dazzle shots in this transcript and none in the control. The results for the hits and misses were equally striking. He found only a few misses in his own transcript and a large number of misses in the control. He found many hits in his own transcript and not a single one in the control transcript. Given this "unanticipated replication," the authors hail the results as compelling support for their survival hypothesis. However, for anyone trained in statistical inference and experimental methodology, this will appear as just another blatant attempt to snatch victory out of the jaws of defeat. . . .

> *The studies were methodologically defective in a number of important ways.*

Schwartz claims that the rater bias could not have affected the ratings of this double-blind experiment. A look at GD's dazzle shots and his discussion of the hit and miss data suggests otherwise. His first dazzle shot is "Bob or Robert." These names occur early in the reading in a statement that goes, "And then I could feel like what I thought was like a divine presence and the feeling of a name Mary or Bob or Robert." This appears in a context with other names and other general statements . . . . The second dazzle shot is "George." Again this appears in a context with no hint that this could be referring to the sitter. Campbell states, "I got like some names like a Lynn, or Kristie, a George." His third dazzle shot is the statement, "I had the feeling of a presence of an Aunt." GD identifies this aunt as his aunt Alice, although Campbell does not provide the name Alice anywhere in the reading. I count at least twenty-seven names thrown out by Campbell during this second reading. Actually, she covers a much broader range of names because she typically casts a wide net with statements like: "And an 'M' name. More like a Margaret, or Martha, or Marie, something with an 'M.'" It is up to the sitter to find a match. As indicated by his dazzle shots, GD is strongly disposed to do so. . . .

## No real scientific evidence

Again, I suspect that Schwartz will disagree with my interpretation. After all, he has already gone on record that this study "provided incontrovertible evidence in response to the skeptics' highly implausible argument against the single-blind study that the sitter would be biased in his or her ratings (for example, misrating his deceased loved ones' names and relationships) because he knew that this information was from his own reading." Nevertheless, the data are quite consistent with the possibility that all we have to do to account for his "breathtaking" findings is to assume that they are due to rater bias.

So what is the bottom line? *The Afterlife Experiments* describes a program of experiments described in four reports using mediums and sitters. The studies were methodologically defective in a number of important ways, not the least of which was that they were not double-blind. Despite these defects, the authors of the reports claim that their mediums were accessing information by paranormal means and that . . . the mediums are indeed in contact with the departed friends and relatives of the sitters. Schwartz's demand that the skeptics provide an alternative explanation to their results is clearly unwarranted because of the lack of scientifically acceptable evidence. A fifth report describes a study that was designed to be a true double-blind experiment. The outcome, by any accepted statistical and methodological standard, failed to support the hypothesis of the survival of consciousness. Yet the experimenters offer the results as a "breathtaking" validation of their claims about the existence of the afterlife. This is another unfortunate example of trying to snatch victory from the jaws of defeat.

# 10

# Apparitions Are a Product of the Imagination

## Joe Nickell

*Joe Nickell has worked as a stage magician, private investi-
gator, journalist, and university instructor. He has a PhD
from the University of Kentucky and is the author of sixteen
books, including* Inquest of the Shroud of Turin, Secrets
of the Supernatural, Looking for a Miracle, Entities, Psychic Sleuth, *and* The UFO Invasion. *He currently works as
a paranormal investigator and writes the "Investigative
Files" column for* Skeptical Inquirer *magazine.*

There is no credible scientific evidence that the dead return to haunt the place of their death. Some "hauntings"
are merely the witnesses' imaginations or daydreams.
Others are a product of the power of suggestion: People
think they see a ghost because they have been told an
area is haunted. Sometimes people who want to perpet-
uate a belief in ghosts create hoaxes. All hauntings can be
refuted with simple explanations.

If testimonials in countless books and articles are to be believed, spending the night in a quaint old hotel might provide an encounter with an extra, ethereal visitor.

Over nearly thirty years of paranormal investigation, I have
had the opportunity to experience many "haunted" sites. These
have included burial places, like England's West Kennet Long
Barrow (where I failed to see the specter of a "Druid priest" that
allegedly attends the ancient tomb); religious sanctuaries, such

Joe Nickell, "Haunted Inns: Tales of Spectral Ghosts," *Skeptical Inquirer*, vol. 24,
September/October 2000, pp. 17–21. Copyright © 2000 by the Committee for the
Scientific Investigation of Claims of the Paranormal. Reproduced by permission.

as Christ Church Cathedral in Fredericton, New Brunswick, Canada (where the apparition of the first bishop's wife did not materialize); theaters, including the Lancaster (New York) Opera House (where a ghostly "Lady in Lavender" was a no-show); houses, like the historic residence of William Lyon Mackenzie in Toronto (where ghostly footfalls on the stairs were actually those of real people on a staircase next door); and other sites, notably inns—the subject of this investigative roundup. (Most of the inns cited—all personally investigated—included an overnight stay, staff interviews, background research, etc.)

> **"** *Research data demonstrates that ghostly perceptions often derive from daydreams or other altered states of consciousness.* **"**

Why haunted inns? Obviously, places open to the public have more numerous and more varied visitors, and hence more opportunities for ghostly experiences, than do private dwellings and out-of-the-way sites. And inns—by which I include hotels, motels, guest-houses, bed-and-breakfasts, and other places that provide overnight lodging—offer much more. They not only allow extended time periods for visitors to have unusual experiences but also ensure that the guests will be there during a range of states from alertness through sleep. Almost predictably, sooner or later, someone will awaken to an apparition at his or her bedside.

## Waking dreams

The experience is a common type of hallucination, known popularly as a "waking dream," which takes place between being fully asleep and fully awake. Such experiences typically include bizarre imagery (bright lights or apparitions of demons, ghosts, aliens, etc.) and/or auditory hallucinations. "Sleep paralysis" may also occur, whereby there is an inability to move because the body is still in the sleep mode.

A good example of an obvious waking dream is reported by "A.C." She was asleep on board the *Queen Mary*, the former ocean liner that, since 1971, has been permanently docked at Long Beach, California. As the woman relates:

> I awoke from a deep sleep around midnight. I saw
> a figure walking near my daughter's sleeping bag
> toward the door. Thinking it was my sister, I called
> out. There was no answer. It was then that I no-
> ticed my sister was lying next to me. I sat up in bed
> and watched the person in white walk through the
> door! . . .

To be sure, not all sightings of ghostly figures are of the
waking-dream variety, many in fact occurring during normal activity. Some are like the report of "J.M." who was at the *Queen
Mary*'s Purser's Desk when, he stated, "I caught a brief glimpse
out of the corner of my eye, of someone or something moving,"
or like that of "P.T." who said, "I saw something move out of the
corner of my eye . . . a brief glimpse of someone or something."
Actually, the illusion that something is moving in the periph-
eral vision is quite common. The typical cause may be a
"floater," a bit of drifting material in the eye's vitreous humour,
although a twitching eyelid, or other occurrence is also possible.

## Daydreams

Such an illusion or a different stimulus—a noise, a subjective
feeling, etc.—might trigger, as in one experiencer aboard the
*Queen Mary*, a "mental image." In that case it was of a man
"wearing a blue mechanic's uniform"—a "feeling" which left
after a few moments. In certain especially imaginative individuals the mental image might be superimposed upon the visual
scene, thus creating a seemingly apparitional event.

This may be the explanation for a frequently reported type
of apparition that is seen momentarily and then vanishes
when the percipient looks away for an instant. For example, a
New Mexico hotel, La Posada de Santa Fe—which is allegedly
haunted by the spirit of Julie Staab (1844–1896), wife of the
original builder—offers no fewer than three sightings of this
type. One was reported in 1979 by an employee who was cleaning one night. Although the place was deserted he looked up
to see a translucent woman standing near a fireplace. Inexplic-
ably, he "returned to his cleaning," an act that one writer noted
showed "remarkable composure." Then, "when he looked up
again the figure had vanished." On another occasion a security
guard showed less reserve when, seeing what he thought was
Julie, "He turned and ran, and when he looked back, the figure

had vanished." Yet again, a "beautifully dressed" Julie, reposing in an armchair, was seen by the hotel phone operator. However, "When she looked back at the chair a few seconds later, the ghost had vanished." Such reports suggest that the apparition is only a mental image that occurs in a kind of reverie.

> *The power of suggestion can help trigger ghostly encounters.*

Indeed, personal experience as well as research data demonstrates that ghostly perceptions often derive from day-dreams or other altered states of consciousness. [Researcher E.] Haraldsson (1988) for instance specifically determined that apparitional sightings were linked to periods of reverie. As well, Andrew MacKenzie (1982) demonstrated that a third of the hallucinatory cases he studied occurred either just before or after sleep, or while the percipient was in a relaxed state or concentrating on some activity like reading, or was performing routine work. The association of apparitional experiences with a dream-like state was also reported by G.N.M. Terrell. He observed that apparitions of people invariably appear fully clothed and are frequently accompanied by objects, just as they are in dreams, because the clothing and other objects are required by the apparitional drama. The three La Posada encounters are consistent with all of these research observations. That the apparitions vanish when the observer's gaze is shifted could be explained by the hypothesis that the reverie is merely broken.

Whereas "waking-dream" type encounters are obviously more likely to be experienced by hotel guests rather than employees, the reverie or daydream type is often reported by the latter—as in all three of the La Posada examples, as well as some of the instances from the *Queen Mary* and elsewhere. Hotel staff performing routine chores may be particularly susceptible to this type of apparitional experience.

## Power of suggestion

The power of suggestion can help trigger ghostly encounters. According to noted psychologist and fellow ghostbuster Robert A. Baker, "We tend to see and hear those things we believe in."

Even without the prompting that comes from an inn's reputation for being haunted, the mere *ambiance* of places with antique architecture and quaint decor can set the stage for spirits to debut. An example is Belhurst Castle, a turreted stone inn in Geneva, New York, whose high-ceilinged lobby is graced with wood paneling, a large fireplace, and a suit of armor to help conjure up romantic notions. . . .

The influence of setting and mood on reports of phantoms is sometimes acknowledged even by those who approach the subject with great credulity, although they may interpret the linkage differently. Broadcaster Andrew Green, for example, in his treatise *Haunted Inns and Taverns*, says of some copies of English pubs in Europe, the United States, and elsewhere: "A few have reproduced the ambiance so successfully that ghostly manifestations, such as might be associated with a genuine article, have occurred there." Green opines that the "genial atmosphere" of such taverns attracts authentic English ghosts. He seems not to consider the possibility that the setting merely influences the imaginations of those making the reports.

## Fact or fancy

In contrast is the knowing statement of ghost hunter Mason Winfield—referring to the allegedly haunted Holiday Inn at Grand Island, New York—that "The environment of the Inn is not the gloomy, historic sort that puts people in mind of spooks." As one who has spent an uneventful night in that resort hotel, indeed in its reputedly most-haunted room 422, I quite agree. But apparitions can occur anywhere. The Holiday Inn's child ghost "Tanya" apparently originated with an impressionable maid who was cleaning the fourth-floor room shortly after the hotel opened in 1973. The housekeeper suddenly glimpsed a little girl standing in the doorway and, startled, dropped a couple of drinking glasses. When she looked up again, the child was gone. As the maid tried to flee, it was reported, "somehow her cart trapped her in the room. She screamed." Her apparitional encounter seems consistent with the typical conditions we have already discussed: at the time, she was performing routine chores. As to the cart, most likely, flustered, she merely encountered it where she had left it, blocking her flight, and panicked.

Other sightings there—like that of a Canadian man who awoke to see a little girl at the foot of his bed—were of the waking-dream variety. But why is it often a little girl even if varyingly identified as age "five or six" or "about age 10"? Those knowing about "Tanya" before their sighting may thus be influenced, while those who do not may, in light of subsequent statements or leading questions from those to whom they report an incident, reinterpret a vague sense of presence or a shadowy form as the expected ghost child. To compound the problem, many of the reports are at second- or third-hand, or an even greater remove. . . .

## Ghosts are good for business

Several inns I have investigated have featured ghosts in their promotional materials. In addition to Belhurst Castle, they include the Hotel Boulderado, the Hollywood Roosevelt Hotel, and Gettysburg's Historic Farnsworth House Inn. The latter advertises that it is "open for tours and ghost stories": "Descend the staircase into the darkness of the stone cellar. Hear, by candlelight, tales of phantom spectres whom [*sic*] are still believed to haunt the town and its battlefield." These storybook ghosts may be the only ones to inhabit the inn. The owner told me emphatically that he had never seen a ghost—there or anywhere else. "I don't believe in that stuff," he said. His daughter, however, who manages the inn, is not so skeptical, having "felt" a "presence" there. She related to me the experience of one guest who had seen a spectral figure after having gone to bed—very likely a common waking dream.

> *Several inns I have investigated have featured ghosts in their promotional materials.*

The effect of new ownership has seemingly launched many hotel hauntings. Stories of ghostly events on the *Queen Mary* did not surface until after the ship became a tourist attraction in 1967. At many other hotels, alleged paranormal events have seemed to wax and wane with changes in management. At the Holiday Inn on Grand Island, for example, the ghost tales—beginning soon after the initial opening—were happily related by one manager. He told a ghost hunter, "Our housekeepers have stories about Tanya that could fill a book." But a successor was "concerned with trying to improve the reputation of his hotel and dispel the rumors surrounding it," refusing "to acknowledge any paranormal happenings."

> *There are no haunted places, only haunted people.*

Ghost tales may indeed be good for business. Explained an owner of one restaurant with bar, which "had a reputation for having ghosts." "It was good conversation for the kind of business we're in. I never tried to dissuade anyone." Other proprietors may go even further. An alleged ghost at the Kennebunk Inn in Kennebunk, Maine, may have originated with the purchase of the inn by one of its earlier owners. He reportedly told a bartender one night that he was "going to make up a story about a ghost," presumably to promote the inn. Years later the former bartender related the story to the current owner, who in turn told me.

## Hoaxes

A hoax could well explain the "ghostly activity" at the Kennebunk Inn, which included "moving and flying crystal goblets, exploding wineglasses behind the bar, disarrayed silverware, and moving chairs." In fact, prior to the particular change of ownership that seemed to spark the poltergeist effects, apparently "all was quiet" at the historic inn. Apparently the ghost moved away when, after about fifteen years, the business was sold again. Still later owners John and Kristen Martin, reopened the inn in mid-1997 and, along with a tenant who had lived there for twenty years, reported no experiences.

Hoaxes do occur. For example, I caught one pranking "ghost" *flagrante delecto.* In 1999 I accompanied a teacher and ten high school students from Denver's Colorado Academy on an overnight stay in a "haunted" hotel. Located in the Rocky Mountains, in the old mining town of Fairplay (where an art teacher conducts "ghost tours"), the Hand Hotel was built in 1931. In the early evening as we gathered in the lobby beneath mounted elk heads and bear skins, the lights of the chandelier flickered mysteriously. But the teacher and I both spied the surreptitious action of the desk clerk, whose sheepish smile acknowledged that one brief hotel mystery had been solved.

Other signs of pranking there included a "ghost" photo (displayed in a lobby album) that the clerk confided to me was staged, and some pennies, placed on the back of a men's room toilet, that from time to time would secretly become rearranged to form messages—like the word "why?" that I encountered. This obvious running prank invited other mischief makers (like one student) to join in. . . .

Over nearly three decades of ghost investigating I have noticed a pattern. In interviewing residents or staff of an allegedly haunted site, I would usually find a few who had no ghostly experiences—for example a bell captain at La Fonda Inn in Santa Fe who had spent forty-three years there. Others might have moderate experiences—like hearing a strange noise or witnessing some unexplained physical occurrence such as a door mysteriously opening—that they attributed to a ghost. Often, those interviewed would direct me to one or more persons whom they indicated had had intensive haunting encounters, including seeing apparitions. In short, I usually found a spectrum that ranged from outright skepticism to mediumistic experiences. I also sensed a difference in the people: some appeared down-to-earth and level-headed, while others—I thought—seemed more imaginative and impulsive, recounting with dramatic flair their phantomesque adventures. I had no immediate way of objectively measuring what I thought I was observing, but I gave it much thought.

At length I developed a questionnaire that, on the one hand, measures the number and intensity of ghostly experiences, and, on the other, counts the number of exhibited traits associated with fantasy-proneness. Tabulation of a limited number of questionnaires administered thus far shows a strong correlation between these two areas—that, as the level of haunting experiences rises, the fantasy scale tends to show a similarly high score.

As this and other evidence indicates, to date there is no credible scientific evidence that inns—or any other sites—are inhabited by spirits of the dead. As Robert A. Baker often remarks, "There are no haunted places, only haunted people."

# 11

# Children's Memories of Past Lives Are Evidence of Reincarnation

## Ian Stevenson

*Ian Stevenson is a professor of research in psychiatry at the University of Virginia. His research interests include children who claim to remember past lives, near death experiences, and survival of the human personality after death. He has written several books, including* Children Who Remember Previous Lives: A Question of Reincarnation.

For decades Ian Stevenson has studied children who claim to remember past lives. These children are young, and no one has suggested to them that they may have been reincarnated. In addition, all of the children make statements that they could only have known by living previously. The children who remember past lives come from many countries, which suggests that there is no cultural bias in their beliefs. Their evidence supports the possibility of reincarnation.

I value . . . highly the spontaneous utterances about previous lives made by young children. With rare exceptions, these children speak of their own volition; no one has suggested to them that they should try to remember a previous life. And at the young age when they usually first speak about the previous lives their minds have not yet received through normal channels much information about deceased persons. Moreover, we can usually make a satisfactory appraisal of the likelihood that they have obtained normally whatever information they communicate about such persons. For the past thirty years I have concentrated my attention on the cases of these young children. . . . I shall present [a few] typical cases, the subjects of which were all young children when they first spoke about previous lives. . . .

## The case of Gopal Gupta

Gopal Gupta was born in Delhi, India, on August 26, 1956. His parents were members of the lower middle class with little education. They noticed nothing unusual about Gopal's development in infancy and early childhood.

Soon after Gopal began to speak (at the age of between two and two and a half years), the family had a guest at their house, and Gopal's father asked Gopal to remove a water glass that the guest had used. Gopal startled everyone by saying: "I won't pick it up. I am a Sharma." (Sharmas are members of the highest caste in India, the Brahmins.) He then had a temper tantrum in which he broke some glasses. Gopal's father asked him to explain both his rude conduct and his surprising explanation for it. He then related many details about a previous life that he claimed to remember having lived in the city of Mathura, which is about 160 kilometers south of Delhi.

Gopal said that in Mathura he had owned a company concerned with medicines, and he gave its name as Sukh Shancharak. He said that he had had a large house and many servants, that he had had a wife and two brothers, and that he had quarreled with one of the brothers, and the latter had shot him.

> *[Gopal] then related many details about a previous life that he claimed to remember.*

Gopal's claim to have been a Brahmin in the previous life explained his refusal to pick up the water glass, because Brahmins would not ordinarily handle utensils that a member of a lower caste had already touched. His own family were Banias, members of the businessmen's caste.

Gopal's parents had no connections with Mathura, and his utterances about a life there stirred no memories in them. His mother did not wish to encourage Gopal to talk about the previous life he was claiming to remember, and at first his father felt indifferent about the matter. From time to time, however, he told friends about what Gopal had been saying. One of these friends vaguely remembered having heard about a murder in Mathura that corresponded to Gopal's statements, but this did not stimulate Gopal's father to go to Mathura and verify what Gopal had been saying. Eventually, he went to Mathura (in 1964) for a religious festival, and while there he found the Sukh Shancharak Company and queried its sales manager about the accuracy of what Gopal had been saying. What he said impressed the manager, because one of the owners of the company had shot and killed his brother some years earlier. The deceased man, Shaktipal Sharma, had died a few days after the shooting, on May 27, 1948.

> *[Victor Vincent] said that she would recognize him (in his next incarnation) by birthmarks on his body.*

The manager understandably told the Sharma family about the visit of Gopal's father. Some of them then visited Gopal in Delhi and, after talking with him, invited him to visit them in Mathura, which he did. At the times of these meetings in Delhi and Mathura, Gopal recognized various persons and places known to Shaktipal Sharma and made additional statements indicating considerable knowledge of his affairs. The Sharma family found particularly impressive Gopal's mention of an attempt by Shaktipal Sharma to borrow money from his wife; he had wished to give this to his brother, who was a partner in the company but a quarrelsome spendthrift. Shaktipal Sharma hoped to mollify his demanding brother by giving him more money, but his wife did not approve of appeasement, and she refused to lend her husband the money. The brother became increasingly angry and then shot Shaktipal. The details of these domestic quarrels were never published and were probably never known to persons other than the family members concerned. (The murder itself was widely publicized.) Gopal's knowledge of these matters, his other statements, and some of his recognitions of persons known to Shaktipal Sharma con-

vinced members of the Sharma family that he was Shaktipal
Sharma reborn.

Along with his statements about the previous life, Gopal
showed behavior that a wealthy Brahmin might be expected to
show but that was inappropriate for his family. He did not hes-
itate to tell other family members that he belonged to a caste
superior to theirs. He was reluctant to do any housework and
said that he had servants for that. He would not drink milk
from a cup anyone else had used.

Dr. Jamuna Prasad, who worked with me for many years on
cases in India, began the investigation of this case in 1965. I
took up the investigation in 1969, when I had interviews with
members of both families concerned, in Delhi and Mathura. I
remained in touch with the case until 1974.

Gopal never expressed a strong desire to go to Mathura,
and after he had been there in 1965, he never asked to return.
For a few years after 1965, he occasionally visited Shaktipal
Sharma's two sisters, who lived in Delhi. Then all contact between the two families ceased. As Gopal became older, he
slowly lost his Brahmin snobbishness and adjusted to the mod-
est circumstances of his family. He gradually talked less about
the life of Shaktipal Sharma, but as late as 1974 his father
thought that Gopal still remembered much about it.

Gopal's case seems to me a strong one with regard to the
small chance that he could have obtained normally the knowledge he had about the life and death of Shaktipal Sharma. It is
true that Shaktipal Sharma belonged to an important family in
Mathura, and his murder was prominent news when it happened. However, the Sharmas and the Guptas lived in widely
separated cities and belonged to different castes and economic
classes. Their social orbits were totally different, and I have no
hesitation in believing members of both families who said that
they had never heard of the other family before the case
developed.

## The case of Corliss Chotkin, Jr.

This case started with a prediction by an elderly Tlingit fisher-
man (of Alaska), Victor Vincent, who told his niece, Irene
Chotkin, that after his death he would be reborn as her son. He
showed her two scars from minor operations, one near the
bridge of his nose and one on his upper back; and as he did so
he said that she would recognize him (in his next incarnation)

by birthmarks on his body corresponding to these scars.

Victor Vincent died in the spring of 1946. About eighteen months later (on December 15, 1947), Irene Chotkin gave birth to a baby boy, who was named after his father. Corliss Chotkin, Jr., had two birthmarks, which his mother said were exactly at the sites of the scars to which Victor Vincent had drawn her attention on his body. By the time I first examined these birthmarks in 1962, both had shifted, according to Irene Chotkin, from the positions they had had at Corliss's birth. Yet they remained quite visible, and the one on Corliss's back impressed me strongly. It was an area on the skin about three centimeters in length and five millimeters in width; compared with the surrounding skin it was darker and slightly raised. Its resemblance to the healed scar of a surgical wound was greatly increased by the presence at the sides of the main birthmark of several small round marks that seemed to correspond to positions of the small round wounds made by needles that place the stitches used to close surgical wounds.

> *He spontaneously recognized several persons whom Victor Vincent had known.*

When Corliss was only thirteen months old and his mother was trying to get him to repeat his name, he said to her petulantly: "Don't you know who I am? I'm Kahkody"; this was the tribal name Victor Vincent had had. When Irene Chotkin mentioned Corliss's claim that he was Kahkody to one of her aunts, the latter said that she had dreamed shortly before Corliss's birth that Victor Vincent was coming to live with the Chotkins. Irene Chotkin was certain that she had not previously told her aunt about Victor Vincent's prediction that he would return as her son.

When Corliss was between two and three years old, he spontaneously recognized several persons whom Victor Vincent had known, including Victor Vincent's widow. Irene Chotkin said that he also mentioned two events in the life of Victor Vincent about which she did not think he could have obtained information normally.

In addition, Corliss showed several behavioral traits corresponding to similar ones that Victor Vincent had shown: Corliss combed his hair in a manner closely resembling the style of Victor Vincent; both Corliss and Victor Vincent stuttered; both had a strong interest in boats and in being on the water; both had strong religious propensities; and both were left-handed. Corliss also had a precocious interest in engines and some skill in handling and repairing them; his mother said he had taught himself how to run boat engines. It is unlikely that Corliss inherited or learned this particular skill from his father, who had little interest in engines or skill with them.

After the age of about nine, Corliss made fewer remarks about the previous life he had seemed to remember earlier, and by 1962, when I first met him, he said that he remembered nothing about it. I met Corliss and his family three times in the early 1960s and once more in 1972. At the time of this last meeting, Corliss had almost completely lost the stuttering that formerly afflicted him, but he still stuttered when he became excited. His interest in religion had diminished, but he had maintained his interest in engines. During the Vietnam War he had seen combat as an artilleryman, and a shell bursting near him had damaged his hearing. Otherwise, when I last saw him in 1972, he enjoyed good health and was working contentedly at a pulp mill near his home in Sitka. . . .

## The case of Shamlinie Prema

Shamlinie Prema was born in Colombo, Sri Lanka, on October 16, 1962. Her parents lived in Gonagela, a town about sixty kilometers south of Colombo, and Shamlinie grew up there.

Shamlinie's parents noticed that even before she could speak, she showed a remarkable fear of being bathed; she resisted with screams and struggling any attempt to immerse her in water. She also showed, while still an infant, a severe phobia of buses, and she cried whenever her patents took her on one, or even when she only saw one at a distance. These phobias puzzled her parents, although they surmised that they might have derived from traumatic events in a previous life.

After Shamlinie began to speak, she gradually told her parents, and other interested persons, about a previous life that she claimed to remember. This life had taken place in a nearby village called Galtudawa, about two kilometers from Gonagela. Shamlinie mentioned the names of the parents she said she had had there, and she often referred to her "Galtudawa mother." She also spoke of sisters and two school companions.

She described the house of the previous life, the location and characteristics of which were quite different from those of the house in which her family was living. She described the death in the previous life in the following way. She said that she went to buy bread in the morning before going to school. The road was flooded. A bus splashed water on her and she fell into a paddy field. She threw up her arms and called "Mother." After that she fell into sleep.

> *A large crowd gathered there when they learned that a child who claimed to have been reborn was visiting the village.*

A girl named Hemaseelie Guneratne, who had lived in Galtudawa, had drowned on May 8, 1961, in circumstances corresponding to Shamlinie's description. (She appears to have stepped back to avoid a passing bus and fallen into a flooded paddy field.) Hemaseelie had been a schoolgirl of just eleven years when she drowned. Shamlinie's parents were distantly related to the Guneratnes, but they had little acquaintance with them and had never met Hemaseelie. They remembered hearing about Hemaseelie's death and feeling sad about it at the time, but afterward they had completely forgotten the incident, and when Shamlinie first began to talk as if she remembered drowning in a previous life, they did not initially connect her statements with Hemaseelie's drowning. However, at about three years of age Shamlinie recognized one of Hemaseelie's cousins when she saw him in a street in Gonagela. More than a year later, she recognized one of Hemaseelie's sisters, also in Gonagela. In the meantime, Shamlinie had been clamoring to be taken to Galtudawa, particularly to visit her "Galtudawa mother," and she compared her own mother unfavorably with the "Galtudawa mother."

Shamlinie's father finally took her to the Guneratne home in Galtudawa. A large crowd gathered there when they learned that a child who claimed to have been reborn was visiting the village. The presence of many strangers may have inhibited Shamlinie so that she made fewer recognitions than she might have done in a more relaxed atmosphere. Shamlinie's father said that she had recognized Hemaseelie's mother, W.L. Podi

Nona, but the Guneratnes remained doubtful about this. The visit, however, permitted verification of Shamlinie's statements, nearly all of which corresponded to facts in Hemaseelie's life. In addition, the two families exchanged information about the girls concerned and learned that Hemaseelie and Shamlinie had some traits in common, such as preferences for certain foods and styles of clothing. . . .

After her first visit to Galtudawa, Shamlinie exchanged some further visits with the Guneratnes, but these gradually diminished over the ensuing years. The decrease in visits coincided with a gradual fading of Shamlinie's memories of the previous life. . . .

Shamlinie's case seems to me to be another one of at least moderate strength with regard to the chance that she had obtained her knowledge of Hemaseelie's life by normal means. It had the undoubted weakness that the families concerned lived within about two kilometers of each other and had had a slight acquaintance before the case developed. In my judgment, however, the rare contacts the families had had could not explain Shamlinie's detailed knowledge of Hemaseelie's life or the unusual behavior that accorded with her statements about it. . . .

## Reincarnation remains a mystery

That is all I can say about evidence we have of the effects in one life from causes in a previous one, and I may have said too much. I think it appropriate to end . . . with an acknowledgment of our ignorance, even with an emphasis on it. Although the study of the children who claim to remember previous lives has convinced me that some of them may indeed have reincarnated, it has also made me certain that we know almost nothing about reincarnation.

# Organizations to Contact

The editors have compiled the following list of organizations concerned with the issues debated in this book. The descriptions are derived from materials provided by the organizations. All have publications or information available for interested readers. The list was compiled on the date of publication of the present volume; names, addresses, phone and fax numbers, and e-mail and Internet addresses may change. Be aware that many organizations may take several weeks or longer to respond to inquiries, so allow as much time as possible.

**The Academy of Religion and Psychical Research (ARPR)**
PO Box 614, Bloomfield, CT 06002-0614
(860) 242-4593
e-mail: bateyb@infionline.net • Web site: www.lightlink.com

The Academy of Religion and Psychical Research was founded in 1972. Its purpose is to encourage dialogue, exchange of ideas, and cooperation between clergy and academics of religion and philosophy. The academy sponsors conferences and symposia for the presentation of scholarly data, points of view, and interchange of ideas in the area where religion and psychical research interface. The academy publishes a scholarly quarterly, the *Journal of Religion and Psychical Research;* a quarterly newsletter, the *ARPR Bulletin;* the proceeding's of their annual conference; and *Inspirational Religious and Spiritual Stories.*

**After Death Communications Research Foundation (ADCRF)**
PO Box 23367, Federal Way, Washington, DC 98093
fax: (253) 568-7778
e-mail: adcrf@adcrf.org • Web site: www.adcrf.org

ADCRF is dedicated to those who have experienced after-death communications with loved ones and to assist in their search for meaning and understanding in the loss of their loved ones. ADCRF is also dedicated to the deceased, whose messages from beyond teach us life continues after death. ADCRF welcomes and encourages all people of all backgrounds, nationalities, countries, and religions to read and participate on their Web site, which lists personal experiences of communicating with the deceased.

**American Society for Psychical Research, Inc. (ASPR)**
5 W. Seventy-third St., New York, NY 10023
(212) 799-5050 • fax: (212) 496-2497
e-mail: aspr@aspr.com • Web site: www.aspr.com

ASPR was founded in 1885 by a distinguished group of scholars who wished to explore the uncharted realms of human consciousness. For more than a century, ASPR has supported the scientific investigation of extraordinary or as yet unexplained phenomena that have been called psychic or paranormal. In addition to laboratories and offices, ASPR maintains a one-of-a-kind library and archive. ASPR serves as a global information network for public and professional audiences. ASPR publishes the quarterly *Journal of the American Society for Psychical Research*.

**College of Psychic Studies**
16 Queensberry Pl., London SW7 2EB
+44 (0)20 7589 3293 • fax: +44 (0)20 7589 2824
e-mail: admin@collegeofpsychicstudies.co.uk
Web site: www.psychic-studies.org.uk

Founded in 1884, the College of Psychic Studies is an educational charity seeking to promote spiritual values and a greater understanding of the wider areas of human consciousness. The college assists individuals in learning about spirituality, including past-life experiences, and by offering numerous lectures, workshops, special events, and healing programs. The college also publishes books through its publishing house, Light Publishing, and prints articles in its journal, *Light*.

**Committee for the Scientific Investigation of Claims of the Paranormal (CSICOP)**
PO Box 703, Amherst, NY 14226
(716) 636-1425 • fax: (716) 636-1733
e-mail: info@csicop.org • Web site: www.csicop.org

Established in 1976, the committee is a nonprofit scientific and educational organization that encourages the critical investigation of the paranormal, including the existence of life after death. The organization then shares the factual information about the results of these investigations with the public and the scientific community. CSICOP publishes *Skeptical Inquirer* magazine.

**Foundation of Thanatology**
630 W. 168th St., New York, NY 10032
(212) 928-2066 • fax: (718) 549-7219

This organization of health, theology, psychology, and social science professionals is devoted to scientific and humanist inquiries into death, loss, grief, and bereavement. The foundation coordinates professional, educational, and research programs concerned with mortality and grief. It publishes the periodicals *Advances in Thanatology* and *Archives of the Foundation of Thanatology*.

**Ghost Research Society**
PO Box 205, Oak Lawn, IL 60454-0205
e-mail: dkaczmarek@ghostresearch.org
Web site: www.ghostresearch.org

The Ghost Research Society was formed as a clearinghouse for reports of ghosts, hauntings, poltergeists, and life after death encounters. The society members actively research and investigate all reports that come their way including private homes and businesses. The society also analyzes alleged spirit photographs and video and audio tapes that they come across from ordinary people or society members. The society publishes *Ghost Trackers Newsletter*.

**International Association for Near-Death Studies (IANDS)**
PO Box 502, E. Windsor Hill, CT 06028-0502
(860) 644-5216 • fax: (860) 644-5759
e-mail: office@iands.org • Web site: www.iands.org

IANDS is a worldwide organization of scientists, scholars, and others who are interested in, or who have had, near death experiences. It supports the scientific study of near death experiences and their implications, fosters communication among researchers on this topic, and sponsors support groups in which people can discuss their near death experiences. The association publishes the quarterly newsletter *Vital Signs* and the annual *Journal of Near-Death Studies*.

**International Association for Regression Research & Therapies, Inc. (IARRT)**
PO Box 20151, Riverside, CA 92516
(909) 784-1570 • fax: (909) 784-8440
e-mail: info@iarrt.org • Web site: www.iarrt.org

IARRT (founded as APRT—Association for Past Life Research and Therapies) is a nonprofit organization dedicated to increasing the acceptance and use of professional and responsible past-life regression through education, association, and research. IARRT publishes the *Journal of Regression Therapy*, which presents research findings and case histories about reincarnation and past lives.

**International Foundation for Survival Research (IFSR)**
PO Box 6152, San Rafael, CA 94903-0132
(415) 499-7731
Web site: www.expbeyond.org

The International Foundation for Survival Research is a nonprofit, tax-exempt organization dedicated to public education about personal experiences and research suggesting consciousness beyond death. IFSR's second purpose is to support ongoing survival research around the world. Several types of research hold much promise for increasing our understanding of the human consciousness and its ability to withstand and survive physical death.

**International Survivalist Society (ISS)**
e-mail: contact@survivalafterdeath.org
Web site: www.survivalafterdeath.org

The International Survivalist Society was founded by Thomas Jones of Wales and David Duffield of West Virginia in April 2002, with the aim of publishing articles, books, and photographs relating to survival after death and psychical research. It is an independent nonprofit organization which regularly cooperates with many distinguished psychical researchers and parapsychologists across the globe. Articles can be viewed on the society's Web site.

**James Randi Educational Foundation**
201 SE Twelfth St. (E. Davie Blvd.), Fort Lauderdale, FL 33316-1815
(954) 467-1112 • fax: (954) 467-1660
e-mail: jref@randi.org • Web site: www.randi.org

The James Randi Educational Foundation is a not-for-profit organization founded in 1996. Its aim is to promote critical thinking by reaching out to the public and media with reliable information about paranormal and supernatural ideas so widespread in our society today. The foundation offers a $1 million prize to any person or persons who can demonstrate any psychic, supernatural, or paranormal ability of any kind under mutually agreed upon scientific conditions. The foundation supports research into the paranormal and publishes the results in their newsletter, *Swift.*

### Ontario Consultants on Religious Tolerance (OCRT)
PO Box 27026, Frontenac Post Office, Kingston, ON K7M 8W5 Canada
fax: (613) 547-9015
e-mail: ocrt2@religioustolerance.org
Web site: www.religioustolerance.org

The Ontario Consultants on Religious Tolerance attempts to serve the people of the United States and Canada in three areas: disseminating accurate religious information; exposing religious fraud, hatred, and misinformation; and disseminating information on dozens of "hot" religious topics. Their goal is to present, compare, and contrast all sides to each issue in religion. The OCRT Web site contains over twenty-five hundred essays and menus on the beliefs of various religions.

### Rhine Research Center
2741 Campus Walk Ave., Bldg. 500, Durham, NC 27705
(919) 309-4600 • fax: (919) 309-4700
e-mail: info@rhine.org • Web site: www.rhine.org

The Rhine Research Center was originally associated with Duke University as an on-campus center of parapsychology experiments. Today the center still participates in research into the unknown. The *Journal of Parapsychology* was established in 1937 to share experimental parapsychological research findings with the scientific community and is still printed by the Rhine Research Center twice a year.

### Skeptics Society
PO Box 338, Altadena, CA 91001
(626) 794-3119 • fax: (626) 794-1301
e-mail: skepticmag@aol.com • Web site: www.skeptic.com

The Skeptics Society is a scientific and educational organization of scholars, scientists, historians, magicians, professors and teachers, and anyone curious about controversial ideas, extraordinary claims, revolutionary ideas, and the promotion of science. Their mission is to serve as an educational tool for those seeking clarification and viewpoints on those controversial ideas and claims. The Skeptics Society sponsors a monthly lecture series at the California Institute of Technology in Pasadena, California, and publishes *Skeptic* magazine.

### Society for Scientific Exploration
Department of Astronomy
PO Box 3818, Charlottesville, VA 22903-0818
(434) 924-7494
Web site: www.scientificexploration.org

The primary goal of the international Society for Scientific Exploration is to provide a professional forum for presentations, criticism, and debate concerning topics in controversial areas and topics that fall between the cracks of traditional disciplines. The society is developing and implementing plans for new educational and research programs. The society publishes the *Journal of Scientific Exploration*.

# Bibliography

## Books

George Anderson
and Andrew Barone

*Lessons from the Light: Extraordinary Messages of Comfort and Hope from the Other Side.* New York: Berkeley, 2000.

John Ashton
and Tom Whyte

*The Quest for Paradise: Visions of Heaven and Eternity in the World's Myths.* San Francisco: HarperSanFrancisco, 2001.

Robert Todd Carroll

*The Skeptic's Dictionary.* Hoboken, NJ: John Wiley and Sons, 2003.

George Dalzell

*Messages: Evidence for Life After Death.* Charlottesville, VA: Hampton Roads, 2000.

John Edward

*One Last Time: A Psychic Medium Speaks to Those We Have Loved and Lost.* New York: Berkeley, 2000.

Bill Guggenheim and
Judy Guggenheim

*Hello from Heaven! A New Field of Research.* New York: Bantam, 1999.

Melvin Harris

*Investigating the Unexplained.* Amherst, NY: Prometheus, 2003.

Karl Jansen

*Ketamine: Dreams and Realities.* Sarasota, FL: Multidisciplinary Association for Psychedelic Studies, 2001.

Eric R. Kandel,
James H. Schwartz,
and Thomas M.
Jessell, eds.

*Principles of Neural Science.* 4th ed. New York: McGraw-Hill, 2000.

James R. Lewis

*The Death and Afterlife Book: The Encyclopedia of Death, Near Death, and Life After Death.* Detroit, MI: Visible Ink, 2001.

Raymond Moody

*Life After Life: The Investigation of Phenomenon-Survival of Bodily Death.* San Francisco: HarperSanFrancisco, 2001.

Donald Morse

*Searching for Eternity: A Scientist's Spiritual Journey to Overcome Death Anxiety.* Charlottesville: VA: Hampton Roads, 2000.

| Jacob Neusner | *Death and the Afterlife.* Cleveland, OH: Pilgrim, 2000. |
| Dean Radin | *The Conscious Universe: The Scientific Truth of Psychic Phenomena.* New York: HarperCollins, 1997. |
| Joel Rothchild | *Signals: An Inspiring Story of Life After Life.* Novato, CA: New World Library, 2001. |
| Susy Smith | *The Afterlife Codes: Searching for Evidence of the Survival of the Soul.* Charlottesville, VA: Hampton Roads, 2001. |
| Rick Strassman | *DMT: The Spirit Molecule: A Doctor's Revolutionary Research into the Biology of Near-Death and Mystical Experiences.* Rochester, VT: Park Street, 2001. |
| Juliette Wood | *The Celtic Book of Living and Dying.* San Francisco: Chronicle, 2000. |
| Jenny L. Yates | *Jung on Death and Immortality.* Princeton, NJ: Princeton University Press, 1999. |

## Periodicals

| Ascribe Higher Education News Service | "Reading the Minds of the Dead: Afterlife Beliefs May Have a Biological Basis, Says University of Arkansas Psychologist," November 26, 2002. |
| *Atlantic Monthly* | "Hell Is for Other People," January/February 2004. |
| Richard J. Bonenfant | "A Near-Death Experience Followed by the Visitation of an Angel-Like Being," *Journal of Near Death Studies*, Winter 2000. |
| Pravrajika Brahmaprana | "Vedanta: Death and the Art of Dying," *Cross Currents*, Fall 2001. |
| John Elvin | "In Search of the Soul," *Insight on the News*, September 10, 2001. |
| *Entertainment Weekly* | "Tomb Reader: A Man of Grave Expectations Celeb Psychic John Edward Talks to the Dead, but Not Everyone Is Buying His Brand of Good Grief," September 14, 2001. |
| Bryan Farha | "Psychic Dodge Ball: The Sylvia Browne Chronology," *Skeptic*, Summer 2003 |
| S.D. Hales | "Evidence and the Afterlife," *Philosophia*, 2001. |
| Craig R. Lundahl | "A Comparison of Other World Perceptions by Near-Death Experiencers and by the Marian Visionaries of Medjugorje," *Journal of Near Death Studies*, Fall 2000. |

| | |
|---|---|
| *Mademoiselle* | "Stairway to Heaven (Near-Death Experiences)," July 2001. |
| Lisa Miller | "Why We Need Heaven," *Newsweek*, August 12, 2002. |
| Todd Murphy | "The Structure and Function of Near-Death Experiences: An Algorithmic Reincarnation Hypothesis," *Journal of Near Death Studies*, Winter 2001. |
| Joe Nickell | "Haunted Plantation," *Skeptical Inquirer*, September/October 2003. |
| Joe Nickell | "John Edward: Hustling the Bereaved," *Skeptical Inquirer*, November/December 2001. |
| Kenneth Oldfield | "Philosophers and Psychics: The Vandy Episode," *Skeptical Inquirer*, November/December 2001. |
| Martin Patton | "Reincarnation," *Subconsciously Speaking*, July 2001. |
| *People Weekly* | "Across the Great Divide: Skeptics Say Mediums Are Just Telling Ghost Stories, but Their Tales of Talking to the Dead Are Captivating the Public," October 25, 1999. |
| Tom Shroder | "A Matter of Death and Life; Ian Stevenson's Scientific Search for Evidence of Reincarnation," *Washington Post*, August 8, 1999. |
| John G. Stackhouse Jr. | "Harleys in Heaven: What Christians Have Thought of the Afterlife and What Difference It Makes Now," *Christianity Today*, June 2003. |
| James Underwood | "They See Dead People—or Do They? An Investigation of Television Mediums," *Skeptical Inquirer*, September/October 2003. |
| Pim van Lommel et al. | "Near-Death Experience in Survivors of Cardiac Arrest: A Prospective Study in the Netherlands," *Lancet*, December 15, 2001. |
| James VanOosting | "Death and Resurrection," *Humanist*, November/December 2002. |
| Tony Walter and Helen Waterhouse | "A Very Private Belief: Reincarnation in Contemporary England," *Sociology of Religion*, Summer 1999. |
| *Washington Post* | "A Matter of Death and Life (Americans Increasingly Hold Religion-based Belief in Life After Death; Survey by National Opinion Research Center, University of Chicago)," September 16, 1997. |

Ewa Wasilewska          "Nor Shall They Grieve: Death and Afterlife in the Qur'an: Part One," *World & I*, September 2002.

Ewa Wasilewska          "Nor Shall They Grieve: Death and Afterlife in the Qur'an: Part Two," *World & I*, October 2002.

Hugh Westrup            "Dead Wrong: TV Psychic John Edward Says He Sees Dead People. Should You Believe Him?" *Current Science*, December 5, 2003.

# Index